STRATEGY
PEOPLE
IMPLEMENTATION

Taking Strategy to Action Through Effective Change Leadership

Russell King & Steve Glowinkowski

Strategy People Implementation

First published in 2015 by

Panoma Press Ltd
48 St Vincent Drive, St Albans, Herts, AL1 5SJ, UK
info@panomapress.com
www.panomapress.com

Book layout by Neil Coe

Printed on acid-free paper from managed forests.

ISBN 978-1-909623-82-8

The rights of Russell King & Steve Glowinkowski to be identified as the authors of this work has been asserted in accordance with sections 77 and 78 of the Copyright Designs and Patents Act 1988.

A CIP catalogue record for this book is available from the British Library.

DEDICATIONS

Russell and Steve would like to dedicate this book to their respective wives Julia and Margaret and thank them for all their encouragement and support.

TESTIMONIALS

In a business and organizational context in which change is paramount, Glowinkowski and King show how focus, analysis and improvement at the level of individual behaviour can deliver enhanced performance. Based on years of systematic research and face-to-face encounters, the lessons contained in this book are invaluable for any modern organization seeking improvements in its operations and overall performance. A clear demonstration of how attention to the social psychology of work can really make a difference.

Todd Landman, Professor of Government and Executive Dean, Faculty of Social Sciences, University of Essex

How do leaders impact business performance? This is a key question that this book answers with 40 years of research to back up the authors' conclusions. The Blue 4 leadership model is a brilliant balance between conviction (some ways of leading are absolutely better than others) and context (use the Blue 4 version best suited to achieving your strategic objectives).

Eric Olson, CEO, Gillson Partnership

In this transformational book, Steve and Russell provide the reader with a practical toolbox revealing how to deliver profitable change. It provides answers to the many paradoxes we face every day when navigating transition and change. Uniquely it offers the reader a "how to" rather than just a "why." It is a must read for anyone seeking to deliver predictability in times of change.

Derek Peacock, CEO, Future Factory

In a sea of bland and overly simplistic books on change and leadership, this book has a great balance of intellectually rigorous research coupled with very practical models that are easy to use but very powerful in action. Traditional employee engagement methodologies tend to produce overly positive results, the blue four model produces a more realistic picture, the initial results will shock many leaders initially but once understood there is a wealth of practical help in the book. Nobody will pretend that institutional behavioural change is easy but at last here is something incredibly useful.

Richard Beaven, Insurance Operations Director, Lloyds Banking Group

ACKNOWLEDGEMENTS

This book reflects many years of experience of leadership, consultancy and research in the field of change and in particular the process of implementing strategy. We have had the privilege of working with some exceptional organizations and leaders. In addition we have both been continually and unabatedly supported by our respective families in this work. We are immeasurably grateful to all.

We have had fantastic teams supporting us over many years in our work and in particular we would like to acknowledge our current team that has provided help and support in the writing of this book. These include Emma Hibble, Hollie Smith, Cassie Croton, Beryl Mead, Irene Belton and Steve Upson.

We would also like to thank Gary Winter and David Physick. Their help has been immeasurable both in terms of writing this book together with their contribution to the many frameworks and models which we refer to and are indeed utilized in our consultancy work.

CONTENTS

INTRODUCTION

Many books have been written about leadership and change. Airport bookstands are littered with them - some good and some less so. "So why write another?" we asked ourselves. Well, as individuals who had both been practitioners, leaders and consultants, we felt that there was something missing - something that meant that the whole story wasn't quite being told. Frankly, we have become disenchanted having to step over the wreckage of abandoned change programs or careers de-railed by ineffective change management. To be honest, we've also gotten a little sick of the reliance on program management that often appears to subscribe to the view that the difference between success and failure when leading change is the quality of the project plan. Contrary to what appears to be popular belief, leaders can't outsource the responsibility for change leadership to program managers or their like. Certainly such approaches have their place, and certainly programs need to be managed, but they don't replace the need to use the behaviours and practices that we discuss in the chapters that follow. In this book we are setting out a more holistic view of what it takes to create a winning company or organization by focusing on the role of the leader in deciding on, creating and leading effective change. Change not for its own sake but so as to beat the competition.

Our basic hypothesis is that there are behaviours, skills and practices that, when enacted thoughtfully within an organization, make it more likely that the organization will fulfill its objectives. It is common cause that many (perhaps most) change programs don't work or under-deliver - we have read that the failure rate is 70% and our experience suggests that this isn't far wide of the mark. Whatever the precise number, we know that change failure is widespread. It was this waste of energy, waste of resources and the consequent damage done that led us to consider how we could best share what works when leading successful and sustainable change programs.

We believe, based on our own research and extensive work experience, that we know why change programs don't work. This insight encouraged us to develop a coherent and integrated approach to leading change for the purpose of outperforming the organization's competitors.

The speed and pervasiveness of change is a given. It may be speeding up or slowing down. It may be disruptive or discontinuous. But we do know for sure that it is simply an integral part of our lives. Sometimes it produces a tailwind and sometimes it blows hard in our faces. Whichever, because the fundamentals of human nature haven't really changed at all, we contend that the levers we pull to motivate people to want to change or perform or simply give of their discretionary effort are the same as they have always been. Sure, technology may help us move along a bit more rapidly, but while we live in a digital age, the people we lead are essentially analog and need to be managed with just as much thought and care now as they did in the past. We don't advocate that going slow should replace going fast but we do strongly argue that care and attention to the detail of leading people is just as important as it has ever been - perhaps even more so.

If you doubt any of this, just reflect on how you have been led, what makes you give your best day after day, what gets you out of bed in the morning. Has your email, or smartphone or video-conferencing changed that? We doubt it! And we say this as people who are wedded to technology in a significant way - just stand behind us at the airport security line as our briefcases disgorge a laptop, an iPad, an iPhone, a Blackberry and a Kindle and you will see that we are anything but Luddites. Instead, while we have a deep understanding of how technology can be utilized to increase productivity and speed up the mundane, we also understand that technology is not a substitute for quality human interaction and engagement.

The basics of motivated employees in successful organizations haven't really changed. We like to work for businesses whose purpose is clear. We like to work with people whom we respect. We like to carry out work that is relevant and valued. We prefer openness, and honesty. We don't like continually switching direction especially if we don't know why. The personal interaction usually beats the impersonal every time. Effective leaders (we aren't even talking about great ones) understand these things and act accordingly. That the medium may have changed doesn't mean that the needs of the people we lead have changed much at all.

Indeed, because we can communicate rapidly, instantly and widely doesn't mean we should. Speed is not a substitute for thoughtfulness. Speed is not a substitute for plan-fullness. Speed is not the same as velocity. In short, before we accelerate we need to ensure that we really understand the how, why and what of what we are doing. Just as the speed and efficiency of modern cars has grown rapidly over the years, the human characteristics of the driver have not. We don't think any faster, we don't see any better, we don't react any more quickly, and the laws of physics are just the same as they have always been. Sure, we can drive faster but does that mean we should, does it raise the chances of crashing, do we arrive at our destination meaningfully quicker? Chances are, probably not.

To be an effective change leader you first need to understand the conceptual model that we have developed to help navigate through the twists and turns of getting things done better. We call this The Change Route Map which is shown in Figure I below and which we introduce in detail in Chapter 1. We then explain each part of The Change Route Map in the subsequent chapters. This will enable you to dip in and out of the book in a way that makes sense to you - even just to read the parts that are relevant to your particular needs. It would be great if you could find the time to read the whole thing but we have written this book on the assumption that you can't or won't.

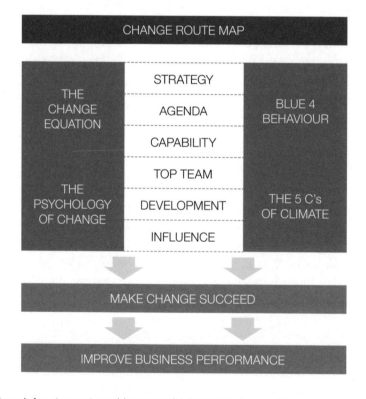

Figure I: A route map to enable successful change implementation

Having explained the Route Map in Chapter 1 we then expand on the Change Equation and its significance in terms of the behaviour and psychology of change. Even if it's a bit heavy-going for some we believe it essential that you understand exactly what it is that gets people to give their best time after time. Certainly, the practices we advocate will help you do that anyway but you will be even more effective, more confident in your behaviours and better able to adapt to unforeseen circumstances if you have a working knowledge of the change aspects of human psychology. Intuitively we all know what makes people "tick" if for no other reason that we are people and we know what makes us tick. If we know this, why do we sometimes think that the workplace is different? The workplace is only different in that it is usually larger and more complex than a social or family situation and this requires us to have a deep understanding of human and organizational psychology.

This psychology of change in Chapter 1 is expanded through Chapters 2 and 3. In all of this we introduce you to the ideas of the Change Equation, Blue 4 behaviour and the Five Cs of Climate change. These are well researched, common sense models that we know work if used properly because we use them ourselves most days of most weeks within our teams and when consulting with other organizations. As W. Edwards Deming (1982) once said, "You don't have to do this, learning is not compulsory, survival isn't either!"

The Change Equation (Figure II) in Chapters 1 and 3 sets out a simple approach for understanding the dynamics of change. While the concept is simple - that the pain of change must be outweighed by the benefits of change for people to want to change - the insights that one gets from using it are very powerful. Is there dissatisfaction with the current state of affairs? Is there a clear vision of the promised land? By which we mean really clear not some fuzzy, fluffy, management aspirational gobbledygook! And is it clear what the first steps or quick wins will be? You really do have to get some quick successes to build momentum. Of course, the sum of the benefits of these three things has to be greater than all the pain of doing it!

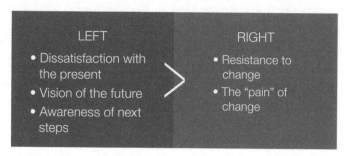

Figure II: The Change Equation

The Model of Behaviour (Figure III) then dives deeper into the behaviours that really deliver the sort of workplace that people enjoy being part of. A place where the leaders are firm and clear about what they want, where feedback is direct and honest but a place where people care about people even if it is sometimes "tough love." We refer to this as Blue 4 behaviour.

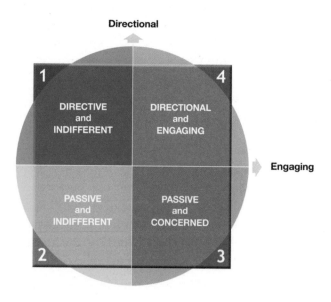

Figure III: The Model of Behaviour

We explore five really important practices that build upon and result from Blue 4 behaviour which helps create the really excellent Climate that distinguishes the great from the average: Clarity of purpose; Commitment from top to bottom; Consistent systems, processes, structures and behaviours; Constancy of purpose and effort; and the Capability to deliver (Table I).

Factors	Meaning
CLARITY	Leaders establish and sustain an environment in their organization in which people clearly understand: • why their organization exists • its purpose • what it is setting out to achieve. People appreciate how, in the short and medium-term, their own work contributes to attaining the longer-term goals.
COMMITMENT	Through their behaviours, Leaders acquire and hold their employees' genuine commitment to the change agenda. People are confident that their organization's Leaders are certain themselves, both individually and collectively, about the change journey on which they wish the organization to embark. As a result, people want the change to be successful and believe they contribute to that success through whatever they do. People feel empowered and able to use their discretion and judgement to improve the quality of what they produce.
CONSISTENCY	For an organization to demonstrate Consistency all aspects of its systems and processes must fit together and be mutually consistent and reinforcing. For example, if Safety is articulated as a top priority both performance management, talent management and reward systems and practices must be consistent with this objective. In short, the organization needs to "walk the talk".
CONSTANCY	Leaders are prone to getting bored, diverted or thinking prematurely that they accomplished their mission. But driving through change requires a long-term constancy of purpose. Change Leaders have to stick to the task and not declare victory too soon - in essence, "they keep on keeping on".
CAPABILITY	For change to be embraced employees need to believe that their organization is truly up to it. People need to feel that there are a minimum of obstacles/hurdles in making the change happen and that the right skills are in place together with employees willing to demonstrate readiness and enthusiasm for change. And they need to believe that the organization will devote the resources necessary to effect the required change.

Table I: The Climate Dimensions

In the last half of the book (Chapters 4 to 10), we address the practices that are required to develop a change program. Deciding what to do - Strategy and Gap Definition (in Chapters 4 and 5), becoming an Effective Change Leader and Getting the Team On Board (Chapters 6 to 8), and Developing an Effective Influencing Strategy (Chapter 9). These represent practical tools and techniques for setting out the change agenda. And finally, Chapter 10 provides an overall summary.

CHAPTER 1

The Change Equation and Blue 4 Behaviour

Before reliable maps were available, those who set out on long and complicated journeys were termed explorers and rightly so. They had only a vague idea where they were going. They had little idea how long it would take, the precise route was ill-defined and the failure rate was high. The spectacularly notable early explorers such as Marco Polo, Vasco da Gama, Christopher Columbus and Sir Francis Drake became successful due to undoubted skill plus a hefty dose of luck. Today, true explorers are few and in business there really is no case for "bet the company" exploration at all.

As business leaders we don't need to set out without a clear idea of where we are going, roughly how long it will take to get there and some clear idea of the costs and benefits of making the journey. It is indeed true that as we navigate, others (our competitors perhaps) are trying to re-draw the map in their favor but that fact places a higher (not lower) premium on the skills of navigation or, as we call it in business, leadership.

The Route Map for Change is a pre-journey checklist and a navigation reference tool. It doesn't replace your own industry "map." It can't locate your business on the map, it won't pick out a desirable destination or checkpoints on the journey, but it will help you ensure that you have minimized the chances of setting out while leaving members of the party behind, either mentally or physically.

First, though, let us return to the issue of speed of change. Frankly, we aren't sure whether change is speeding up or slowing down - does it matter, would it be different if we knew which, and how can you measure it anyway? All we can be reasonably certain about is that change is a fact of life, it isn't going away and so we might as well embrace it and ride the wave. The aforementioned explorers, whether Marco Polo in the C13th, Columbus and da Gama in the C15th, or Drake in the C16th would doubtlessly also have said that the world was changing pretty quickly and quite unpredictably. And in their case, it wasn't just technology but also radical changes in ideas and understanding of the world as well. Something that is not nearly as pervasive or destabilizing for us today.

In his book *Good Strategy/Bad Strategy*, Richard Rumelt (2011, p.179) says:

"Business buzz speak constantly reminds us that the rate of change is increasing and that we live in an age of continual revolution. Stability, one is told, is an outmoded concept, the relic of a bygone era. None of this is true. Most industries, most of the time, are fairly stable. Of course, there is always change, but believing that today's changes are huge, dwarfing those in the past, reflects an ignorance of history."[1]

Exactly!

And, we might add, whatever our attitude to change, we ignore at our peril that the fundamentals of human nature are essentially the same now as they were in Drake's day. Whatever else has happened, the psychology of the human condition hasn't changed. Like it or not, we are the same now as we ever were.

We may be better educated, we may be wealthier, better nourished, fatter, thinner or more worldly-wise but our psychology is pretty much unchanged. And to add to Rumelt's (2011) comments, to think otherwise doesn't just betray a fundamental ignorance, it also consigns us to getting leadership very wrong!

Nor does the pervasiveness or use of technology change this one little bit. Sure it helps us get things done more quickly, and it does create new opportunities for interaction, but the people we lead need to be managed with just as much thought and care as they ever have. We don't advocate

---

1   *Good/Strategy/Bad Strategy, Richard Rumelt 2011, Profile Books, page 179*

that going slow should replace going fast but we do strongly believe that care and attention to the detail of leading people is just as important as it ever has been (perhaps even more so).

As we said in the Introduction, if you doubt any of this, just reflect on your experience of how you have been led, what makes you give your best day after day, and what gets you out of bed in the morning. The basics haven't really changed. We all thrive when the purpose of what we do is clear and we respect the people we work with. We like to carry out work that is relevant and valued. We prefer openness, and honesty.

We don't like continually switching direction, especially if we don't know why. Effective leaders understand these things and act accordingly.

What do we mean by change? The term is used frequently. A Google search brings up more than 4 billion references. There's a lot of information about change, but what does it mean and how do we use the term?

Nadler and Tushman (1989) define it on two dimensions:

- Scope: Incremental or Strategic
- Timing: Reactive or Preemptive

and further refine this definition to provide four typologies:

- Adaptive - an incremental change that is reacting to an external stimulus such as the removal of lead in gas in response to medical research that it was harmful to children.

- Re-creation - a strategic change in response to an external stimulus such as the development of "bricks and clicks" retailing in response to the evolution on the internet-only stores.

- Fine-tuning - making incremental change in anticipation of an external development such as the gradual phasing out of solvents in painting materials in anticipation of changing environmental legislation.

- Re-orientation - strategic (usually step) change in anticipation of an external development such as the early outsourcing of production to low-wage economies to secure competitive advantage.

Our view of Nadler and Tushman's (1989) categories is that beyond their academic relevance, they challenge us to consider the degree to which we wish to be proactive or reactive, and the degree to which we wish to evolve or make step changes. While the situation of the organization will usually dictate the best fit answer, it is our view that anticipating the impact of change, embracing it and using it to the advantage of the organization is a preferable attitude. Strong incumbents often find this difficult and many fail or underperform as a result.[2]

While change carries risk, not changing, as Christensen (1997) argues, carries even more. Successful organizations adapt to their changing circumstances and the most successful ones create their own good fortune by changing ahead of the game. The Change Route Map covers the essentials of leading change and is an essential part of the change leader's toolbox (Figure 1.1).

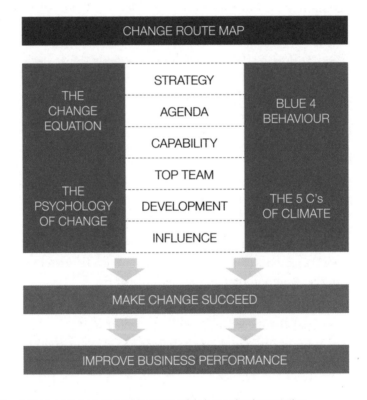

Figure 1.1: A route map to enable successful change implementation

---

2   *The Innovator's Dilemma, Clayton Christensen, HBS Press, 1997*

On the left and right sides of the model we explain the essential concepts that need to be understood to be an effective change leader. While each of the concepts is discrete, our experience suggests that they are all the more powerful if they are combined or used together.

The Psychology of Change

The Change Equation

Blue 4 Behaviour

The Five Cs of Climate

These four factors help reflect the complex dynamic of change and provide considerable insight about why most change programs fail to deliver their promise. From a practical perspective they provide a useful template for any leader wanting to achieve their change objectives. The remainder of this chapter (plus Chapters 2 and 3) provides an integrated account of how these factors fit and link together. The center of the model contains the steps that need to be addressed to actually plan and lead effective change. These are discussed through Chapters 4 to 9.

But change programs don't work, do they?

The overwhelming evidence suggests that change programs typically don't work or at best fail to deliver the initial promise about 70% of the time. There are numerous examples to support this from mammoth initiatives in the UK public sector to the smaller scale examples we see in commercial organizations. Not only is the notion of so much wasted time, effort and money profoundly depressing, it also implies that the activities of most change leaders destroy rather than create value.

Through this book, we provide a toolkit that enhances the likelihood of a change program working. So, we will discuss both what effective change looks like, why it works and describe the most effective levers that result in lasting change and therefore sustainable competitive advantage.

People have a natural resistance to change

In managing change, psychology is a big deal and the better a change leader understands just what makes people tick and why, the better they're going to be as change leaders. Let's start with the primary principles of the critical psychological concepts that help us understand why it is so difficult for change to be managed through to a successful outcome. When talking about change from a people perspective, we are referring to two things: firstly, behaviour in terms of what people do and how they do it and secondly, attitude in terms of what they think and feel about what they do, and their overall values and beliefs.

It is easy to imagine achieving behavioural change quite quickly. People may do as they are told and this may last for a while but without a corresponding shift in attitude it is likely not going to be sustainable. The behaviour will fade at the first opportunity (i.e. when the boss goes on vacation) and will inevitably fail to become the new norm.

At a more personal level, people who go on diets or give up smoking often make an initial change in their behaviour, but if their heart is not in it they soon regress back to the cupcakes or the cigarettes.

In industry, safety performance is a good example. In terms of workplace safety, we can be sure that no one gets up in the morning to go to work with the intention of getting killed or injuring themselves at work and yet so many safety programs set out with great intent and initial behaviour change (i.e. safer performance) but eventually that fades away with time. People "do" the safe behaviour for a while and then revert to type. They fail to make a fundamental change because they don't really believe that anything bad will happen to them. Similarly, we know that driving over the speed limit raises our chances of being harmed if we crash but we ignore this fact because we don't believe that it will happen to us.

This is why achieving sustainable change is so difficult – a change in behaviour is not enough because we also need a shift in the attitudes, values and beliefs of the individuals that the change leader is endeavoring to change. We argue that it is only when the behavioural change is followed by a corresponding change in attitude that you get true "conversion." We also argue that in order to get this conversion it must be preceded by a consistent and positive experience in terms of behavioural change. This issue was very well illustrated by the American psychologist Leon Festinger (1957). Festinger argued that what people do, or more specifically how they behave, tends to shape their attitudes and beliefs. When a mismatch or lack of congruence between behaviours and attitudes occurs then it generates a kind of tension or conflict. He referred to this as Cognitive Dissonance. Put simply, when people are "caused" to behave in a way that is not in accord with their attitudes, values and beliefs it provokes a feeling of dissonance.

The natural human tendency is to remove this dissonance and achieve equilibrium, and the most obvious way to do this is to stop the incongruent behaviour. However, if for some reason the behaviour is maintained or persisted with, then the equilibrium can be achieved by a shift or change in attitude.

In the latter example the individual will become used to the new behaviour. It has become the norm because the attitude has changed. If you like, we could say that we observe a sustainable shift in behaviour, because the individual probably forgets that it used to feel different – it has become the usual way of doing things.

In a very strong sense this mismatch between behaviour and attitude with resulting dissonance is not necessarily a bad thing. Indeed, it can be looked on as a highly positive state. The old behaviour could be negative and the new behaviour represents the way to go. Therefore if we can find a way of ensuring that the new behaviour can persist for a while then it may generate the new positive attitude and belief and thus make the new norm of behaviour both highly welcome and sustainable.

Our position is that the concept of Cognitive Dissonance is the means by which sustainable behavioural change can be achieved. From the perspective of the change leader the critical question is how the right type of dissonance can be created and maintained in order to deliver the required sustainable change.

Festinger was an academic psychologist and as such conducted many interesting experiments which demonstrated this concept. There are, however, many more practical and close to home illustrations which show the power and significance of this link between behaviour and attitude.

Perhaps this was most markedly noticeable during the 1960s and 1970s as racial attitudes changed in the United States due to emerging desegregation. A quite specific example is shown when racial attitudes were measured before and after legislation which outlawed segregation in the transport system of a U.S. city. Following the legislation, racial attitudes on both sides showed highly significant improvement. The key point is that the legislation forced a change in behaviour, i.e. blacks and whites mixed together, the forced change persisted and each group overcame the dissonance through a gradual process of recognizing and realizing more positive attributes than previously imagined. Their behaviours had been changed (through the legislation) and this established dissonance. The dissonance was resolved by a change in attitude toward their fellow citizens. No amount of publicity, chat shows or preaching from academics about the worth of racial equality could have had anything near the same impact on attitudes as an actual change in behaviour did.

More recent work conducted in the UK lends support to the idea that behaviour (or experience) drives attitudes. Nick Vivyan and Chris Hanretty (Hanretty 2014) examined attitudes of people from 632 British constituency boundaries. They found that voters in constituencies with fewer migrants were more likely to hold negative views about immigration. The survey consisted of 30,000 respondents. In other words, those people who lived in areas with a high percentage of migrants tended to have more positive views about whether immigration has a culturally positive impact (quoted by Sam Coats and the Times Data Team in *The Times* newspaper Tuesday, October 21st 2014).

As change leaders/consultants ourselves, we have seen Cognitive Dissonance at work in many major change programs. In a job redesign program involving a confectionery manufacturer we observed a production line change from hierarchical prescription to one of semi-autonomous work groups. The outcome showed an immediate shift in the behaviour of the employees which resulted in an immediate performance improvement. It took a further 18 months to register a significant shift in job satisfaction and well-being.

The change leaders in this job redesign program worked hard to establish an empowering leadership style alongside the restructuring of the roles. First, line supervisors were removed leaving work groups responding directly to shift managers. These managers, in turn, then focused on delivering behaviour with the groups that had an appropriate balance of direction, control and democracy. This on one hand provided the right level of clarity for the workgroups but on the other hand also provided scope for autonomy. The change leaders persisted with their change of behaviour. Consequently the new behaviour of the employees had the time to impact attitudinal states. As a result, we saw a consolidation of the behaviour and attitude and a continuing attitudinal change over the next three years. This seemed to provide a robust underpinning and foundation for the new behaviours. In the end, it was the attitudinal shift that enabled the behavioural change to be sustainable.

At its heart, the theory argues that it is behaviour that drives attitude and that this is time orientated. For attitudes to change the behaviour must be consistent and constant over a prolonged period of time, otherwise there is a risk that old attitudes will stick fast. Change leaders need to find ways that enable an initial shift in employee behaviour which then persists over time to enable a positive attitudinal change to emerge. It is this process of behavioural and attitudinal change that we define as engagement: "They do it and they believe it."

Human nature is such that change in a leader's new "contradictory" behaviour has to persist long enough to cause dissonance in their employee's mind. By continuing to deliver the contradictory behaviours, those people will change their attitudes and regard the previously different behaviours as the norm. By contradictory behaviour we mean quite bluntly the thing that happens which changes the behaviour of the recipients.

These ideas of Festinger reflect the difficulties that we have observed in creating meaningful and sustainable change in organizations. We have found the idea of a Change Equation a very practical way of thinking about what needs to be done if you are going to be able to create sustainable change.

The concept of Change Equation was developed by Gleicher (Beckhard and Harris 1987). It breaks down the essence of making a change into its component parts. The formula states:

Dissatisfaction (D) x Vision of Future (V) x First Steps (F) > Resistance to Change (R)

In summary, therefore: D x V x F > R

In other words, if the resistance to change (or the 'pain' of change) is exceeded by the multiple of current dissatisfaction, the existence of a vision of an alternative state and clarity of what the first steps look like in order to make the vision reality, then the easier it will be for the change to take place. Conversely, where the multiple of the three factors is exceeded by the resistance to change, then the change becomes less of a possibility.

As change leaders ourselves, we have often used this equation to complete a quick diagnosis of the current state of play in an organization about to embark on change. Clearly, if people aren't unhappy with the way things are, have no idea what the future might look like and don't know how to get started then a change program will never even get started. However, often the issues are more subtle or complex than that; a clear vision has been expounded to people within the enterprise and some initial exploratory steps have been taken. But, in the main, people are not that unhappy with the current state so they're not motivated in themselves to become more deeply involved and increase those first steps into longer strides.

Alternatively, people may well be unhappy with their current state and can't determine an alternative way. There is no vision and therefore no initial first step. They don't quite know what to do first or are anxious about initiating that first move. This of course emphasizes the change leader's role in providing the direction or way forward in terms of a new and compelling vision. This provides a clear sense of why the change is important and how the individual will perform in the longer term direction.

In addition to the "why" individuals need clarity about the practical next steps that need to be taken. The wise change leader is likely to provide this but also recognizes that the recipients of the change are likely to possess great insight themselves about what these next steps might be. They just need to be encouraged to contribute their ideas.

To overcome any resistance to change, it is necessary for all three components of the left-hand side of the equation to be strong. Simple perhaps, even obvious; plain common sense in reality. Yet, it is something we see continually overlooked, ignored or forgotten. The equation itself does not provide the answer to creating an effective change program; however, understanding its precept is fundamental to appreciating the potential issues concerning building momentum and conviction about the reason and necessity to make the proposed changes. It is often said that leaders need good followers and that is precisely what the Change Equation is all about; how can a leader expect anyone to follow them if they don't know where they are going, they don't want to go there and, in any event, they don't know how to start the journey?

Before we go further, let us amplify this point a little more as it is important to emphasize that change is something about which organizational leaders really need to "get real." There is no silver bullet or magic wand that makes the change occur miraculously overnight. There is a logical process to be followed and believing that everyone is prepared to take a huge leap into the dark is the stuff of fantasy.

A further consideration for the change leader is that there are important individual differences in terms of how people react to change. We can represent this difference as a continuum of incremental versus radical thinking style. Incremental thinkers enjoy change which is practical and step by step. Radical types like change which is big and dramatic. The majority of the population is neither strongly incremental nor radical; they are somewhere in between.

As such, change proposals that are dramatically radical, e.g. whatever we have we will dispense with and start afresh, or incremental, e.g. we intend to "have the drains up" and explore every finite area of detail, are going to be more likely to be resisted. Gaining buy-in will be far harder in such instances. Interestingly, we find that most change leaders tend to be strongly radical in their predisposition to thinking. Consequently we often observe both the change that they like, together with how they communicate it, emphasizes the radical style of thinking. In the context of the Change Equation this can present a major problem in appealing to the change followers who are more likely to veer toward the incremental end of the thinking style continuum. In practical terms this probably means a fundamental communication issue with the change followers failing to appreciate the articulated direction and key next steps by the change leader. We will come back to this issue of thinking predisposition in more detail later on in the book.

In organizations, if change leaders want to change the attitudes of their employees, e.g. to believe that great customer service makes a difference at both the level of reputation and financial performance, they have to change behaviours, not least their own. For example, having a boss "go off" about customer service who refuses to talk to an angry customer simply undermines the whole change program – change leaders have to "walk the talk" and preferably "walk the walk." Witnessing a failure of deeds to match words, employees are likely to revert to previous ways because that is congruent with the boss's actual behaviour. People are very smart at observing what goes on and often take more clues from this than from what is being said. They are "anthropologists" possessing shrewd insights about the true culture of the place as opposed to the corporate propaganda espoused through posters, DVDs and intranet portals. When leading change, it is imperative that leaders never forget that people look at what they do more so than listen to what they say.

Johnson and Scholes (2006) pointed out that employees listen to what bosses recount in their "war stories"; for instance, do they talk about something that is absolutely central to the organization's purpose or do they talk about the CEO's largess at the time the party line is frugality? Do they talk about lack of respect, mistrust, people being badly treated despite senior managers pontificating about respect? Does the organization's safety or environmental record evidence congruence or dissimilarity with what is communicated? Jim Collins (2009) in his book *How the mighty fall: and Why Some Companies Never Give In* highlights the potential death knell for organizations when leaders' own hubris drowns out all the other messages – sound familiar?

Considering these primary psychological factors is crucial at the outset and throughout managing any change program. They do not concern being "nice" or taking a benign approach. Tough issues still have to be confronted and resolved. However, if they are done so in a manner which creates and manages dissonance ineffectively, the likelihood of the change being completed and producing the projected benefits will recede rapidly. The consequence is severe because such failure means the receptivity to another piece of change will be lower; the "we've tried that, it didn't work" syndrome materializes.

In the course of Chapters 2 and 3, we shall revert in more detail to these concepts and they will re-appear many times during our ongoing narrative.

How to make change happen effectively

If economics is the "dismal science" then change appears to be regarded as a "black art" with countless books, articles, conferences, webinars and social networks devoted to the subject. Many make out that change is complicated but it doesn't need to be that way. Good change leaders make complicated stuff simple rather than the other way around! Admittedly, successfully steering a change program through to completion requires a lot of attention to detail, hard work, commitment and determination. It requires agility to deal with the unexpected "balls from left-field" that are encountered. Certainly it is rare in our experience that a change program proceeds in an orderly, linear fashion. The basics of conducting efficient and effective change, like human nature, as we will discover later in the book have not changed in the course of hundreds of years!

As we stated in the Introduction, the fundamental hypothesis of this book is that effective, purposeful and sustainable change is dependent upon five interconnected factors that combine to form the organizational environment, for which we use the term Climate. By this we mean "how it feels to work around here," i.e. the perception of the people who work there. Remember, "Perception is Reality."

In short, we are considering whether people are in themselves motivated by and committed to what they experience at work or is work something about which they are at best indifferent, at worst complacent? In this sense, Climate is a much more sophisticated way of thinking about culture because it considers the human factor far more explicitly than tends to be the case ordinarily when looking at culture as "the way things are done around here." If the way things are done is felt to be inspiring and motivational, there will be a far healthier Climate than if this is not the case.

How do we create an effective Climate? How do we ensure that all the pieces of the Climate jigsaw fit together? How do we explain Climate to those we lead? Tough questions indeed, but the five factors we describe have the great virtue of being memorable, effective, necessary and sufficient.

Climate comprises five critical features.

CLARITY	Employees possess a clear sense about where the organization is heading and where they fit into that direction
COMMITMENT	There is a feeling of full engagement where employees feel a sense of commitment and pride to be part of the organization's direction
CONSISTENCY	There is a sense of alignment and consistency that senior management and their employees are all pulling in the same direction
CONSTANCY	There is a sense of persistence and constancy that behaviour maintains its direction, focus and purpose over time - things stay on track
CAPABILITY	There is a sense that the organization has the capability, resources and drive to achieve its goals

Table 1.1 The Five Critical Features of Climate

This framework is defined in much greater detail in Chapter 2, but for the moment we define these five constructs of Climate in Table 1.1.

The second aspect of our hypothesis concerns how this type of Climate or environment is created and we position this directly at the feet of the change leader. It is fundamental to the role of the change leader (indeed anyone in a leadership position) that their role is to establish and set the conditions, in part through how they behave and in part through how they manage the organization generally in a way which establishes what we call a Climate of real performance orientation. The behaviour of the change leader creates the Climate which in turn establishes the conditions required which enable effective behaviour and attitude change to emerge in the organization as a whole.

In one project we worked with a large group of back office administrators from a financial services organization. This involved running a series of brainstorming workshops with over 500 staff (in groups of 10-22). In the workshop sessions we asked the question "If you could change three things in this company what would you change?" The response was amazingly consistent, where over 90% of responses could be positioned in terms of the following three categories:

- Clearer direction of where the company is heading

- Performance management that helps me perform effectively and provides feedback

- Collaboration within and between teams

So, what change followers expect from change leaders is direction and engagement – the boss needs to point the direction and show that they are interested in them. Indeed, even when there is a crisis, say a storm at sea, the followers expect the leader to be tied to the wheel to provide direction and show that they care about the crew, not reading charts below in the cabin.

This simple role definition is reflected in our behavioural framework that was briefly outlined in the Introduction. It consists of two simple dimensions. The first is about the change leader setting the direction and way forward (Directional) and the second is about the change leader engaging, listening and focusing on the change followers (Engaging).

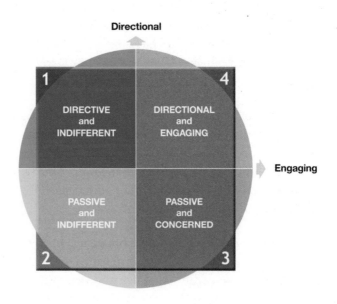

Figure 1.2: The Model of Behaviour

The framework is shown in Figure 1.2. The vertical axis positions Directional behaviour. The horizontal axis positions Engaging behaviour. The resulting two-by-two matrix presents four color-coded quadrants and going anti-clockwise they are Red, Amber, Green and Blue 4.

Red is Directional but not Engaging behaviour. In this a way forward is provided but the change leader demonstrates no interest in the thoughts and the views of the change followers. This style of behaviour is likely to be perceived at best as impatient and disinterested in the views of others and at worst authoritarian and coercive. Because the behaviour of the leader is also poor on Engagement, the directional component will be experienced as highly Directive thus the label is "Directive and Indifferent."

Green behaviour is Engaging with others but lacks a Directional component. It is thus non Results Focused in approach. In this the change leader expresses no view about the way forward but shows a great deal of interest in the thoughts, views and feelings of the change followers. This style of behaviour is likely to be perceived as very friendly and affiliative but without any drive, focus or intent about what needs to be achieved. This lack of direction causes the "people behaviour" to be perceived as Concern for Others rather than Engaging with others. Hence the label in Green is "Concerned and Passive."

Amber behaviour lacks both Directional and Engaging behaviour and is seen and experienced by others as Indifferent and Passive. In this the change leader expresses no view about the way forward and shows no interest in the thoughts and views of the change follower. This style of behaviour is likely to be perceived as entirely aloof and disengaged from the world of the change follower.

Blue 4 behaviour is Directional and Engaging. In this the change leader provides direction about the way forward with a sense of focus in addressing issues that need to be addressed. They also demonstrate engagement and therefore an interest in the views, thoughts and feelings of the change followers.

It may seem obvious that Blue 4 is the behaviour that leaders always need to deliver. After all, it's hard to imagine any change follower being impressed by an assertion from a change leader if that leader showed no interest in them, i.e. they were indifferent. Equally, it would be hard to imagine a change follower being satisfied with their leader if they were interested and concerned in them but showed little sense of what they wanted them to do, i.e. their leader was passive with little or no results focus.

Red and Blue behaviour is equally Directional. The only difference is that the Blue 4 leader combines with that direction, interest and concern for the change followers. This causes the leader's input to be perceived as Directional rather than Directive in style. Blue and Green are equally concerned or engaged. The difference is that the Blue 4 Leader combines with their Concern for Others a way forward – the Direction. In this context Concern for Others will be seen and experienced by the change as truly Engaging behaviour.

With Blue 4 there are many different behaviours that emphasize/include all the components of Blue 4 (e.g. Results Focus, Interpersonal Awareness, Strategic Thinking, Developing Others etc). In Chapters 6, 7 and 8 we will explore these components in more detail in both an individual and team context. At this stage, however, we ask you to think Blue 4 as the effective combination of all behaviours that will underpin a Directional and Engaging approach. We label Blue as Blue 4 behaviour because we refer to four fundamental contexts in which leaders need to operate:

1. The setting of direction and objectives

2. The communication and influence process

3. The driving of performance and decision making

4. The management of performance and development of others

In Chapter 6 we will explain how the Blue 4 framework represents a high level overview or aggregate of a more detailed behavioural specification.

Blue 4 behaviour represents the type of culture which creates a Climate of Clarity, Commitment, Consistency, Constancy and Capability. This sets the right environment or conditions for change. It encourages and enables behavioural change in the change followers to be persisted with and thus helps attitudes to change. It is fundamental in creating sustainable change.

We have worked with and assessed well over 50,000 change leaders from across sectors and cultural/geographic regions. We have conclusive data that shows Blue 4 behaviour as a driver of the Five Cs of Climate. We refer to Blue 4 behaviour as the idea of Blue 4 culture, i.e. it reflects what can happen in an organization, what the behaviour is like and how things get done. It manifests the idea of a culture where both the behaviour and practices of the change leader provide Direction and Engagement. It is a mechanism which manages the complex psychological dynamic of the Change Equation. It is the way that dissonance can be created and maintained in a positive way such that its eventual erosion helps create a new and positive norm of behaviour and attitude (Figure 1.3).

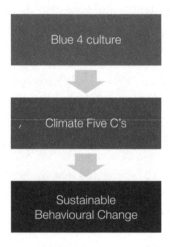

Figure 1.3: the flow of Behaviour through to sustainable change

In this chapter we have discussed the change concept in terms of what change is, why it is important and yet why it is so difficult to achieve. We finally presented an overview of what change leaders need to do in order to realize sustainable change.

The next two chapters explore in greater detail the fundamentals of this model.

CHAPTER 2

Climate and Blue 4 Behaviour

Our opening chapter made four points:

- Although change is a prime requirement for all organizations, most interventions fail to deliver on their promise.

- Change interventions fail because the critical requirements of the Change Equation have not been met and as a consequence sustainable behaviour and attitude change in the change followers is not achieved.

- To manage change effectively change leaders need to create the right conditions for change in terms of establishing the Five Cs of Climate in terms of Clarity, Commitment, Consistency, Constancy and Capability.

- These conditions for change can be established by the change leader through both their own behaviour and the manner in which they deliver their accountabilities. We refer to this behaviour as Blue 4. It is Blue 4 which establishes the conditions for change, i.e. the Five Cs of Climate. The Five Cs are the "what" and Blue 4 is the "how."

In the next two chapters, we will explore more fully the people issues that need to be considered by managers initiating change and to use this understanding to raise the likelihood of people "getting with the program." To achieve this, change leaders must behave in such a way that they create an Organizational Climate in which their employees also become motivated to support change, either by being directly involved in its implementation or being ready and willing to accept the new way of working. So with this in mind, let us explore the organizational characteristics that managers need to create and exploit positively if their change agenda is to prove successful.

Quite simply, for change to be implemented successfully it is essential that change leaders create a strong and healthy Climate within their enterprise – because it is this, and this alone, that has the effect of engaging people, which in turn motivates them to deliver their discretionary effort. When the Climate is positive people go the extra mile for themselves, their colleagues, their boss and their customers (see Figure 2.1).

Figure 2.1: Link between Climate, Engagement and Performance

In this chapter, we explore the conditions needed for change to occur successfully and how these conditions can be fostered, nurtured and sustained. In so doing, we will touch upon some critical but well-grounded psychological concepts that are fundamental to achieving a good grasp of what it is to manage change successfully.

It is vital that change leaders understand these issues because all too often we find that managers believe that it is the force of personality that drives all before it and that simply by being charismatic, gregarious, ebullient, or tactile they will win people over. While such behaviours may be helpful they are neither necessary nor sufficient for success in managing or leading change. Indeed, to rely on such attributes risks the change leader being regarded as shallow, manipulative and ultimately failing at what they set out to achieve. As we've said before, as people take more meaning from what people do than what they say, the "charismatic" risks building resentment and resistance if those particular gifts are not married to a substantive understanding and deployment of the real levers of change.

Climate

So, just what do we mean by Climate and motivation? And how do they stimulate and drive organizational performance?

Research conducted in 2009 by Glowinkowski International Limited (Glowinkowski 2009), the leadership development consultancy founded by co-author Dr. Steve Glowinkowski, shows that, all things being equal, a positive Climate in an organizational workgroup is a significant driver of superior business performance. By Climate we mean "how it feels to work here"; do people feel committed to their work and are they proud to be working for their organization? (A perception that is affected fundamentally by the behaviours of the organization's leaders). Quite simply, if leaders' behaviour isn't constructive, it is highly unlikely that their employees will feel motivated to act in the best interests of the organization. Conversely, if the leaders behave in the correct manner they will engage more effectively with their employees, which will result in them being more motivated and aligned with the organization's goals. This direct link between behaviour and Climate is summarized in the Integrated Framework as depicted in Figure 2.2

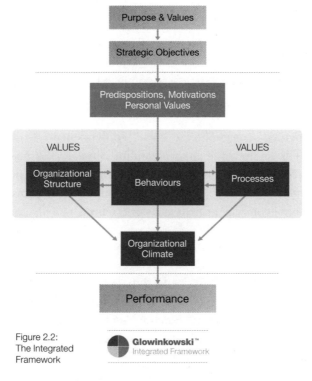

Figure 2.2:
The Integrated
Framework

Glowinkowski™
Integrated Framework

The Integrated Framework defines Climate as the principal driver of outstanding performance in *any* organization. Climate is different from, yet interdependent with, the concept of culture, which we recognize as relating to "how things are done here." Climate can be described as representing the atmosphere or mood of the workplace. This is not to suggest an easy-going environment - far from it. But most importantly, it is an environment in which people are prepared to use all their skills and expertise to drive and raise performance however that is measured.

From Glowinkowski's extensive research and its measurement work with clients, two very clear connections are seen.

1. All things being equal, the quality of a Climate differentiates an average from an outstanding organization, i.e. two apparently similar organizations by, say, size and activity, may be delivering markedly different levels of performance. This is due to the higher performing organization possessing a measurably higher quality Climate.

2. Whatever the level of performance currently being achieved by an organization, effort constructively expended to improve its Climate will improve its performance outcomes. Such investment pays dividends.

3. For example, using the Integrated Framework, one investment option is for leaders to learn to deliver enhanced behaviours. A positive shift in behaviour will deliver a quantifiable improvement in the Climate.

In a commercial enterprise, a clear consequence of this Climate improvement is an increase in profitability. Similarly, in an educational institution, we see Climate growth correlating with improved academic and social performance. What is more, we have seen such improvement occur in times of both economic growth and contraction.

While the Integrated Framework shows Climate as a driver of performance, it also depicts the components of Organization Structure and Processes, alongside the aforementioned leadership behaviours, to be the drivers of Climate. We often refer to these three factors as the change levers of Climate. Collectively, the three levers represent how things get done, i.e. the culture of the organization. *In other words, Climate is an outcome of culture.* It is change levers that represent the culture.

In this context, change levers can also be seen as reflecting the values of the organization. If the espoused values are actually reflected in the way the organization operates then the change levers of Structure, Behaviours and Processes will be effective. This will drive the Climate and subsequent performance.

Climate was initially coined as a concept in the late 1930s by Kurt Lewin and colleagues (Lewin, Lippit and White 1939 also Lewin 1951) in their work with "experimentally created social climates" before becoming used in organizational studies in the 1960s, most notably by Litwin and Stringer (1968) who sought to understand the link between perceived Climate in an organization and the impact on individual motivation. This work has been added to by, among others, Burke and Litwin, Ekval (1987) and, more recently, Goldman (2000).

All the academics mentioned above provide a framework describing the composition of Climate that provides a generic platform on which a debate about the causation of organizational performance can be based.

Our focus, however, is different in terms of it being aimed at the very specific issue of managing the successful implementation of change. We concentrate our attention on leaders creating and maintaining a Climate in which change can be forged, fostered and nourished. Such a Climate comprises five critical conditions or dimensions, which are explained in Table 2.1, and we group together under the Five Cs.

Factors	Meaning
CLARITY	Leaders establish and sustain an environment in their organization in which people clearly understand: • why their organization exists • its purpose • what it is setting out to achieve. People appreciate how, in the short and medium-term, their own work contributes to attaining the longer-term goals.
COMMITMENT	Through their behaviours, Leaders acquire and hold their employees' genuine commitment to the change agenda. People are confident that their organization's Leaders are certain themselves, both individually and collectively, about the change journey on which they wish the organization to embark. As a result, people want the change to be successful and believe they contribute to that success through whatever they do. People feel empowered and able to use their discretion and judgement to improve the quality of what they produce.
CONSISTENCY	For an organization to demonstrate Consistency all aspects of its systems and processes must fit together and be mutually consistent and reinforcing. For example, if Safety is articulated as a top priority both performance management, talent management and reward systems and practices must be consistent with this objective. In short, the organization needs to "walk the talk".
CONSTANCY	Leaders are prone to getting bored, diverted or thinking prematurely that they accomplished their mission. But driving through change requires a long-term constancy of purpose. Change Leaders have to stick to the task and not declare victory too soon - in essence, "they keep on keeping on".
CAPABILITY	For change to be embraced employees need to believe that their organization is truly up to it. People need to feel that there are a minimum of obstacles/hurdles in making the change happen and that the right skills are in place together with employees willing to demonstrate readiness and enthusiasm for change. And they need to believe that the organization will devote the resources necessary to effect the required change.

Table 2.1: The 5 C's of Climate

Clarity

The Clarity that exists within any organization or component unit, function or team provides a sense of purpose or direction. Where Clarity is strong, individuals will understand *what* the organization is trying to achieve or *what* it is trying to change and *how* it intends to complete the change program. This is as much about tomorrow's goals as it is about those that are longer term. Broadly speaking, everyone in the organization must clearly, concisely and precisely understand the goals that affect them day in and day out – where the organization is headed and why. When they do, they will appreciate how *their* work relates to that of *their colleagues* and the *overall* aims of the organization. This fosters the necessary spirit to strive to achieve the common aims. Cutting through the business lexicon of purpose, vision, mission, strategy, goals, aims and objectives, organizations possessing pin-sharp Clarity enjoy the fact that, quite simply, their people understand what is being changed and why! Such people engage with change in a resolute and disciplined way. It is for this reason that Clarity is the single biggest, most important determinant of success in an organization whether in steady-state or change mode. Think about it: how can anybody be committed to anything if they aren't absolutely clear what "it" actually is?

Performance implications of Clarity

- When people work in an organization where Clarity is strong, they know what works well and what doesn't; they know what needs to change and why. They recognize how their own skills, knowledge and experience can contribute toward what needs to be done. They are thus able to contribute to their fullest potential. They volunteer to do things beyond the precise remit of their role; they are truly committed to the cause. Efficiency, productivity and effectiveness all grow.

- The corollary is that without Clarity, people are more likely to pull in different directions and attach varying priorities to activities. People will be inclined to work in their own silos and be less mindful about the consequence of their changing some aspect of what they do.

Of the Five Cs, without doubt, Clarity is the most critical. Without it, the other four dimensions are much diminished in their efficacy.

Commitment

This relates to the extent that leaders have acquired and bolstered people's buy-in to the change agenda. As a result, people are genuinely committed to exploiting their own strengths in order to help their organization carry out its change agenda. They support changing what gets in the way of the organization being more successful. They appreciate such success doesn't come automatically; it has to be strived for. Commitment is hard to win but very easy to lose.

The essence of Commitment is that people understand exactly how they, personally, will benefit from any proposed change – they know "What is In it For Me" (WIFM). In getting to the WIFM it is critical to begin to engage directly with the interests of all levels of the workforce. A miner drilling holes in a dark, wet, hot gallery a couple of kilometers underground is unlikely to relate to an objective to create a world-leading mining company, but he/she might well relate to having secure, safe and remunerative employment for himself/herself and his/her family for years to come. So, it is indeed "different strokes for different folks" and great change leaders understand this and address the issues with this always firmly in mind. It is for this reason that so many corporate videos and posters remain a testament to top management hubris rather than examples of effective employee engagement.

But even creating Commitment by working out WIFM is not always straightforward. Rarely, can Commitment be created by exhortation and rhetoric. Instead, leaders often have to create the necessary conditions that guide people in the right direction. If people are encouraged by the environment in which they work to behave in a certain way then their attitudes will often align accordingly. For example, to get people to put safety first you have to ensure that the disciplinary consequences of them not doing this are clear and implemented consistently.

This is where the earlier mentioned notion of dissonance is important; when people are "forced" to behave in a certain way their attitudes will eventually align or they will leave the organization. Clearly, dissonance for its own sake is unlikely to be positive but it is vital to understand that in managing change it is the "mind" that follows rather than leads the change process.

Performance implications of Commitment

- Change can't happen unless all the people at all levels of the affected organization are positive about it or at least are not going to be fighting against it. If you don't get buy-in (or at least acceptance) at all levels your change program will ultimately fail.

- While we will talk about this more under Consistency, it is vital to ensure that people are encouraged to behave in a constructive way to then enable them to think in a constructive way; people need a framework to aid their understanding and to ensure that it develops in the right direction.

- Commitment needs to be as well developed as possible across the entire organization. Having any significant divergence in the level of Commitment that exists in different parts of an enterprise is dysfunctional as it causes stresses and strains that deflect from the common cause; indeed, in more extreme causes, the non-committed areas can impede, disrupt or undermine change. If apathy rather than Commitment is detected, leaders must change their influencing approach and work out how else they can win buy-in. Simply accelerating pace may not resolve the issue – remember slow is the new fast!

Consistency

To be honest we debated at some length whether we should refer to this attribute as Congruence (i.e. all parts of the system fit together) or Consistency (i.e. all parts of the system are consistent with each other). In the end Consistency won out but we thought we'd mention Congruence just in case it makes more sense to you!

So, Consistency requires that every facet of the change process, the systems underlying the process, the systems governing the organization in general and the behaviour of the leadership team are Consistent with the desired change and with each other. Everything has to be Consistent with everything else. In a sense this is both obvious and often ignored. And often ignored because it is simply pretty laborious to make sure that everything is Consistent; it adds to the workload; it seems bureaucratic and it simply isn't nearly as exciting as the delivering at the town hall meeting, making the video or producing the ad campaign. We agree with this sentiment – ensuring Consistency isn't a lot of fun but the problem is that if you don't do these things people won't believe you are serious. Remember, we have pointed out a few times now that people basically end up believing and signing on to those things that they are encouraged (or even forced) to do. Therefore, if the leader talks about creating a change to a "Safety First" culture but the performance management system rewards production before safety then don't be surprised if production is the top priority. Because, in effect, the reward system is saying "Now I know the guys at the top are blathering on about safety but they don't really mean it because they still reward us on production rather than working safely." Similarly, if despite the safety message the organization still promotes managers with poor safety records, what will their employees think? Certainly not that safety is number one.

Therefore, when starting out on a change project it is really important to examine all the systems and processes that are part of the 'business as usual' rhythm of the organization and ensure that they are absolutely Consistent with and reinforcing of the direction in which you wish to proceed. Yes, it is a pretty tedious part of the process but it is not one that you can short cut or ignore – your people look at what you do, not what you say.

Performance implications of Consistency

- Consistency is crucial to establishing that the change program is serious and is for the long-term. It reinforces the message from every direction and effectively channels behaviour toward the desired outcome. It reinforces Clarity because it ensures that there aren't any misleading or conflicting messages from any part of the system.

- Consistency also demands that the leadership team act consistently with the change process. If safety is important should the boss boast about how fast his new car goes? If people are to be respected should the CFO "ball-out" a subordinate in public? If people are being fired should the board travel First Class? If innovation is being encouraged why is failure so deprecated? We could go on but we guess that you get the message!

Constancy

All too frequently, we see change programs lose momentum because a decision is taken to change course, or to declare victory too soon, or to add another change initiative to the agenda. While successful change programs are not those that "come hell or high water" drive blindly toward accomplishing their original aims despite circumstances altering in such a way that adjustment is needed, they are those which maintain a Constancy of purpose combined with a dexterity to pre-empt or react to external dynamics. Many changes in direction, many early victories and many new add-on initiatives arise, we find, from managers sensing that an initiative has run out of steam and needs re-energizing, or that they have gotten bored or that they genuinely believe that everything has happened when in fact they are simply disconnected with reality. So, rather than being constant of purpose, managers start saying things differently or saying different things or, worse still, doing different things or focusing on different things. The end result is confusion and dimming of Clarity. The result is to cause people to think *Well, if I keep my head down, it'll go away and we'll wait until the next idea comes along*. A change program can quickly peter out and disintegrate if leaders aren't resolute in their focus and determined to leave no stone unturned in their determination to secure the change. Like Consistency, Constancy isn't very exciting but if you don't "keep on keeping on" with the change program, rest assured that nobody else will either.

For managers who are naturally inclined to possess short attention spans or enjoy working with a constant stream of new ideas, any diminution of their focus and attention will, at the most senior level, cause confusion and a decline in Clarity. Again, while any change program needs to be tweaked from time to time, change leaders must be very careful about the consequence of the signals they send as the adjustments are made.

The Constancy dimension emphasizes the criticality of keeping the show on the road over the long-term and not allowing the initial start-up energy to wane. Where a change of course is justified, Constancy reminds people of what overall is being attempted. Constancy provides the determination to re-group and seek an alternative course of action.

Through Constancy, people feel that there is perpetuation and purpose and their attitude changes. Such reinforcement of behaviour is absolutely fundamental particularly in the context of the dissonance theory mentioned earlier. One of the key things in terms of achieving attitude change is the need to maintain the sense of behaviour and approach that you want to prevail. If this occurs then attitudinal change in terms of buy-in will prevail.

How long is long enough? Well, we think that most significant change programs need to be measured in years rather than months. Sure, you will see results more quickly but until the results come day after day, regardless of the change management process, you haven't reached a point of sustainability. In an Australian consumer products company of about 3,000 people it took about three years of constant effort by the leadership team before the shop floor had truly "got it", before they had worked out WIFM and before they owned the change program as much as their leaders.

Performance implications of Constancy

- If people perceive Constancy, they are more likely to change their behaviours and their attitudes. Change is sustainable rather than emerging in fits and starts with the risk that any initial commitment fades at best due to lack of interest and at worst downright cynicism.

- Where a change program contains a sequential series of activities, lack of Constancy will result in people losing interest. Clarity will dim, Commitment will be lost. Consistency and Constancy is required to build and maintain competitive stamina. Without this, even dominant organizations can quickly fade to obscurity.

Capability

The extent to which the organization is up to the change will be instantly understood and appreciated by the change followers. This can be viewed in a number of different ways. The first relates to how easy or difficult it is perceived by the change followers to succeed in trying something new. Often we observe change not happening because people perceive "just too many obstacles" or it is "just too much hassle to get this agreed." Part of an organization's Capability for change relates to the extent to which employees perceive a minimum of obstacles/hurdles in making the change happen. If the organization is seen as fluid and responsive as opposed to bureaucratic/ stifled and serving vested interests, then the change will provide the "heart" for the minds of the change followers. When the "heart" is added to the mind the change followers will feel the emotional buoyancy of "we can do it" instead of the "dead hand" of cynicism.

People are of course realistic and while the perception of minimum obstacles is critical, it is not sufficient. Employees also need to see that the organization has the necessary skills, structures and processes in place that the new change state requires. This aspect of Capability can have a number of themes including the Capability of the top team in so far as they are perceived as the best option available to provide the type of leadership that they require. The formal structures and processes also need to be seen as credible by the change followers and fit the purpose in terms of the task in hand together with the skills, knowledge and experience with the employees who are expected to both implement the change and work with it in terms of business as usual.

A further aspect of the Capability dimension touches on the idea of readiness or enthusiasm for change. Employees or change followers need to believe that their colleagues are up for change, will embrace it and indeed relish the opportunity for improvement. While this may seem somewhat idealistic it is nevertheless a critical strand of the experience of Capability and it furthermore emphasizes the importance of "change capital" that management may have in the sense that too many false change starts will destroy an organization's chances of capturing people's enthusiasm for innovation.

As with each of the other Climate dimensions, Capability is fundamentally driven by the three change levers of Structure, Behaviour and Processes. The change leader needs to utilize these factors because in a Climate of high Capability employees are interested and compelled to improve the work that they do.

Performance implications of Capability

- When people experience a strong level of Capability there is a clear sense of people being able to make improvements. Often this results in the organization demonstrating real adaptability and a deft touch in its customer engagement.

- Because change is regarded as exciting and motivating by the majority of people, they are keen to consider new ways of doing things; they want the organizational culture to change (remember, we distinguish culture as the way things are done, i.e. it relates the organization's systems, procedures, protocols and practices).

- Organizational resources are continually available to facilitate change. This is not to suggest that there are people on standby doing nothing until a change request is initiated but rather that the organization is able to assemble new teams or reallocate resources to different activities with relative ease. Consequently, organizations possess dexterity and momentum to respond quickly to emerging market forces. In the very high-scoring organizations this faculty enables them to pre-empt emerging customer requirements and steal a march on the competition.

Having defined the organizational characteristics that managers need to construct and subsequently manage, in the next chapter we will explore how this Climate affects individuals' motivations and the extent to which they are willingly and positively involved in making their change agenda a success rather than another addition to the long list of failures.

CHAPTER 3
The Psychology of Change

Our premise is that with the Five Cs in place, the resulting Climate means there is far greater chance (although never complete certainty) that individuals involved in delivering a change program will be engaged and motivated to get the job done. This is because when people experience fully the Climate conditions of Clarity, Commitment, Consistency, Constancy and Capability, it is motivating for them and contributes to the energy and drive for them to engage productively in the new and changing environment.

Psychologically the experience of positive Climate reinforces the change followers' motivations to adapt to the dissonance and drive change effectively. This chapter explores the link between Climate and motivation more deeply. Firstly, let's consider the topic of human motivation and exactly how this is driven or encouraged by Climate.

What do we mean by motivation? It is a massive field of research and here we draw out the key elements. There are three principal pillars to human motivation, which are:

- Choice - what someone wants to do

- Persistence – how long they will do it for

- Effort – how hard they will try

To these three pillars we add the following definition of motivation: "A person is motivated by an ongoing desire for a future-state which energizes and orientates their behaviour."

From over a century of extensive research about motivation, we distill the field into six broad approaches, which are summarized in Table 3.1.

The Motive	The Essence of it
NEEDS	Doing the behaviour is satisfying and fulfils an intrinsic need, she therefore does the behaviour.
REINFORCE-MENT	She behaved in a certain way, got rewarded and there-fore repeated the behaviour.
EXPECTANCY	He thought the behaviour would deliver the required result and be valued so delivered the behaviour.
EQUITY	The last time she behaved like that she got what she thought was a fair reward; therefore she did it again.
GOAL	The goal was difficult but not impossible. They persisted and eventually achieved the desired outcome.
SELF EFFICACY	She felt confident in her abilities and really believed she could compete effectively. She ran the race and won.

Table 3.1: Approaches and theories of motivation

Considering each of these in turn, while there are similarities between the six approaches they remain discrete and valid theories and ones which will aid a change leader's understanding of what's involved in motivating people to give of their discretionary effort.

Motivation as Needs

This approach to motivation positions the concept as an aspect of personality, i.e. someone is considered to have a characteristic drive. Two major theories in this field are those of Maslow (1943) and Herzberg (1959).

Maslow talked about a "hierarchy of needs" from basic safety and security through to self-esteem and self-actualization. Herzberg spoke in terms of two dimensions, one being basic satisfiers and the other being higher level motivators. Hence, it is common to encounter people where pay is the satisfier and the social interaction provided by work is the motivator.

Another framework is that of David McClelland (1987) who identified social needs for Achievement, Affiliation and Power. In terms of Achievement, McClelland argued that certain individuals had a high need to outperform against standards of excellence they had set themselves, e.g. the athlete wanting to run or cycle quicker than previously. In terms of Affiliation, a person has a need for harmony in their relationships with other people. And finally in terms of Power, he talked about the need for individuals to be influential and impactful over the behaviour and actions of others as opposed to controlling and demanding, i.e. socialized versus personalized power. By socialized power McClelland meant "influence for the greater good" as opposed to acting for personal self-aggrandizement.

In this approach, an individual has a need for something to be fulfilled or satisfied. If such an opportunity prevails in the environment in which they operate, they will be motivated to engage more fully than if the opportunity were absent. For instance, an individual motivated by Affiliation, i.e. wanting harmony in their relationships or liking to be liked, will be motivated by a situation in which giving love, care and attention is encouraged. A "dog-eats-dog" or "everyone for themselves" environment will not motivate them.

Motivation as Reinforcement

This approach is rooted in behaviourist research conducted by Robert Skinner (1938). At its heart lies the idea of reward and/or punishment as a means of enhancing or reducing the extent to which a particular behaviour is delivered or not. Thus, if a certain behaviour occurs and is rewarded then it is likely to reinforce repeat delivery of the behaviour. Conversely, if the behaviour is in some way punished or negatively reinforced, then the behaviour will be extinguished.

Motivation as Expectancy

Victor Vroom (1964) posited Expectancy Theory, which incorporates three primary factors:

- The first is that an individual believes that increasing their effort will lead to higher performance – this is termed *expectancy*.

- The second is that performing well will lead to receipt of a valued outcome – this is termed *instrumentality*.

- The third is the idea that the outcomes will be valued – this is termed *valence* e.g. offering financial reward to someone who would rather have time off work will not motivate.

All three conditions need to be present and can be summed up as: "Is the extra effort worth the possible benefit?"

Motivation as Equity

Equity Theory was advanced by John Stacey-Adams (1963). Essentially it says, "If I get out of a task what I put in, I'll be motivated." When change leaders get this balance wrong an individual might feel that there is a disequilibrium in their "psychological contract" and this can result in reduced productivity, less care and attention in tasks, work avoidance, and in extreme cases, theft and sabotage.

Motivation as Goal Pursuit

Goal Theory is most strongly associated with Locke and Latham (1990) who purported that setting challenging but realistically attainable goals results in higher performance. Conversely, a goal beyond realistic reach will produce the opposite effect: people will switch off. Interestingly, a target regarded as too easy or soft can have a similarly demotivating effect.

The 80/20 rule prevails. Research shows human beings need to engage in activities that they feel have an 80% chance of success and a 20% chance of failure according to how they view their abilities. Without this trade-off, some people can become stressed, which is known to affect health and well-being as well as productivity.

Motivation as Self-efficacy

The concept of Self-efficacy was promulgated by Albert Bandura (1997) and concerns the idea that individuals believe they can achieve a particular task. Thus, when an individual has high self-esteem, they will feel motivated to try to complete a task successfully. If they fail, they will learn from the experience. Where an individual has low self-esteem, they are more likely to believe they won't be able to complete the task and, if they can, avoid doing it.

How Climate underpins Motivation

As mentioned, we have no intention of reviewing the full field of motivational theory and research; it is too vast and not what we want to focus upon. However, having some understanding of these six approaches is very helpful in determining how they relate to the Five Cs. What conditions need to be set in order to provide the required motivational stimuli to those people who are involved in effecting change in the organization and for those affected by the change?

Figure 3.1 shows a matrix of the Five Cs and the six modes of motivation. Each factor of Climate will have a larger or lesser impact upon motivation from whichever perspective it is considered.

CLIMATE INPUTS	MOTIVE OUTPUTS					
	NEEDS	REINFORCEMENT	EXPECTANCY	EQUITY	GOAL	SELF-EFFICACY
CLARITY	✓	✓	✓	✓	✓	✓
COMMITMENT	✓		✓	✓		
CONSISTENCY		✓	✓	✓		
CONSTANCY			✓	✓	✓	✓
CAPABILITY	✓		✓		✓	✓

Figure 3.1: How Climate impacts Motivation

Examining some of these linkages in more detail, we see:

- Low Consistency and Equity

Low Consistency can be characterized by a sense of people feeling there is one rule for one and another rule for someone else. This disparity will affect the question of "What's in it for me?" in terms of "I do more than her, yet she gets more. I am not going to put in that effort anymore."

- Low Constancy and Expectancy

Through low Constancy, senior managers' enthusiasm for change can dissipate causing employees to wonder: What was all the fuss about? In this context Expectancy theory can account for why these individuals may question whether it is worthwhile their putting in extra effort and, if they do, whether or not managers will value their endeavors.

- Low Commitment and Self-esteem

In a merger between two companies operating in different parts of the financial services market, one company felt as though the other was taking it over, which reduced their Commitment to the deal. The change did not go smoothly and when it was eventually completed late and over budget, the projected benefits failed to materialize. In this context, low levels of Commitment undermined self-esteem. This explains why acquiring companies often fail to capture the potential of the human capital they acquire.

- Low Capability and Needs

In a Climate of low Capability, people with a high achievement motivation will feel little or no opportunity to develop and utilize their skills in a real challenging context. Low Capability Climate also undermines people's self-confidence in their ability to achieve success. In this sense we can see a strong connection between the Climate dimension and the idea of Self-efficacy in terms of motivation. Indeed, the Climate dimension of Capability is probably one of the most significant features that will undermine people's motivation for innovation and creativity.

- Low Clarity

Clarity, as the over-arching and critical component of Climate, has significant impact upon people's motivation from a number of angles. If the reason for the change is not explained, people will feel in a vacuum and thus it reduces self-esteem. Lack of Clarity will not set the right conditions to set challenging goals, which undermines motivating those who have high achievement needs.

Putting it Together

Fundamentally, and we cannot stress this enough, change leaders cannot motivate other people directly. However, they can establish the right conditions, i.e. Climate, in which people motivate themselves to deliver exceptional work. In an environment of change, managers who build and sustain a Climate characterized by strong Clarity, Commitment, Consistency, Constancy and Capability will stand a far better chance of their change program delivering on time, to budget and to intended outcomes.

- Within the Integrated Framework, the change levers of Structure, Behaviour and Processes represent how things are done within an organization - in other words, how the organization behaves.

Great behaviour drives great Climate in terms of how people feel it is like to work there, and strong Climate means better performance.

- Given strong Climate, people will feel more directly engaged with what the organization is trying to accomplish. They will feel motivated to put in extra effort to overcome obstacles, make a difference and help the organization do new things well or existing things better.

- Weak Climate will, at best, result in people "motivated" to deliver the minimum effort required, and at worst to feel alienated or "motivated" to disrupt the workplace.

How this fits with the Change Equation

If, due to a great Climate, the individual feels highly motivated then they will exhibit the drive and energy to persist with their new behaviour and thus overcome their dissonance. In terms of the Change Equation they are likely to experience a higher score on the left-hand side (see Figure 3.2) than on the right-hand side of the equation.

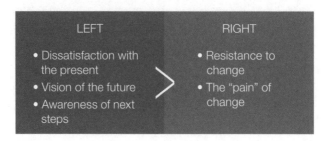

Figure 3.2. The Change Equation

The six frameworks of motivation we have previously discussed represent different aspects or processes of human motivation. Let's consider how these might impact the energy applied or the awareness of the individual with respect to the Change Equation.

- From the perspective of Self-efficacy (Bandura 1997), the individual with high self-belief will be more engaged in order to try it out and, therefore, be prepared to take the first few steps, withstand the initial trepidation of the change and potentially come to see and believe that the pain of the change is not so painful after all.

- In Equity Theory (Adams 1963), the individual recognizes that there is something in all of this hassle for them and it is, therefore, worthwhile going the extra mile. In this instance they are likely to gain a personal dissatisfaction naturally (because they see a personal benefit) with the current state and that will tend to override their extent of personal pain with the change in hand.

- Using Needs Based Theories (Maslow 1943, Herzberg 1959 and McClelland 1987), the individual will recognize that engaging in the change will satisfy their own deep drivers. So, from the point of view of an individual with a high need for achievement (say), the pain of change is diminished because engaging with the change will actually satisfy their own needs in a deep and meaningful way, i.e. the difficulties can be seen as an achievement challenge and therefore an opportunity for personal fulfillment.

- With Goal Theory (Locke and Latham 1990), a well-articulated and understood vision together with clarity about the practical next steps will mean that the goal of change can be seen as both challenging and realistic (perhaps even SSMART: Stretching,

Specific, Measurable, Achievable, Relevant and Timebound). This means that goal-orientated motivation is stimulated because there is an 80% chance of success and 20% chance of failure.

- From a Reinforcement perspective (Skinner 1938), we can imagine that ongoing feedback throughout the new behaviour phase will help individuals stick with the initial difficult early stages of the change transition. This is of course helping to dissipate the feelings or conflict of dissonance mentioned earlier, thus enabling the new behaviour to stick and new attitudes to become established. Recognizing the importance of reinforcement emphasizes the role of the change leader as a coach in terms of a provider of feedback and this helps to diminish the significance of the right-hand side of the Change Equation.

- And finally, from the perspective of Expectancy Theory (Vroom 1964), it is critical that individuals really understand that senior management are serious about the change and mean what they say. This emphasizes the criticality of how the vision is set and the clarity provided in terms of the next steps. If this is effective then people will see what is required and believe it. This of course maximizes the left-hand side of the equation. However, whether management really do mean it will be crucial when the change transition has started, thus requiring constancy and so continuing to help individuals to believe their pain really is worth it. In this context people will stick with it and this emphasizes the right-hand side of the equation.

Change leaders who fail to build and enrich the Climate of their organizations will not succeed in creating the motivational conditions for change to emerge and succeed. In the mind of the change followers, the dominant aspect of the Change Equation will simply be the pain of the change. When this happens, the change leaders have only themselves to blame. Henry Ford once said, "Coming together is a beginning. Keeping together is progress. Working together is success." Climate is entirely concerned with working together in an engaged and collaborative manner.

So change initiatives usually fail due to the following:

- Change leaders not realizing that their primary accountability is to build and sustain a high-performance Climate, one in which change is positively regarded when it is purposeful and objective rather than being done for the sake of it or due to some new fad.

- Too little focus on creating and sustaining a Climate which sets the motivational conditions for the Change Equation to be managed.

The practical and executable side of the Change Equation concerns change leaders creating an environment in which their people:

- Understand their organization's strategy

- See how their work directly contributes to the strategy being achieved

- Know what they have to do, i.e. task, and how to do it, i.e. behaviour

- Have a line-of-sight to the external customer and/or other stakeholders

- Know what needs to happen by when

- Perceive that proposed changes are in everyone's interests, i.e. there is a sense of fairness

- Value the projected benefits of the change over and above the effort or pain they will experience in terms of delivering the change

Change leaders who build a high-performance, change-orientated Climate by focusing on establishing genuine strength of capability across the Five Cs will set the conditions in which their people will motivate themselves to push through the change agenda and create an enterprise that is more competitive and wants to win and be the best in its field.

For attitudes to change, behaviours must be maintained. Changing behaviours represents a change in culture of an organization. Sustaining a change in behaviour invokes a new culture, a new way of doing things. In turn, this brings about a new outcome in terms of an improved Climate: it feels better here. This doesn't mean laid back or even necessarily friendly, but rather that people collectively feel motivated to accomplish more for themselves, their team, their organization, their country. As President J.F. Kennedy (1961) remarked in his inauguration speech, "Ask not what your country can do for you, but what you can do for your country." It concerns producing a condition in which people are keen and willing to devote their discretionary effort to improve the organization. When this happens a virtuous circle of improvement and performance results.

Whenever senior management behaviour regresses, for instance when they revert to coercive behaviour having stated they intend to be more involving and collegiate, Climate will "jump back" to its original position. In fact, in our experience it tends to fall back further because people feel duped or somehow misled. For change to take root fully, change leaders need to ensure they get right the rhythm of their communication. In other words, the Consistency and Constancy dimensions of the Five Cs are crucial.

If this rhythm is robust and in tune, there is less chance of deviant behaviour arising to threaten the desired new attitudes. Get it right first time! Rush things, and mistakes are made and money is wasted.

Is Slow the new Fast?

We have mentioned slow being the new fast a couple of times so far, but is it true - and if so why? Our previous section provided insight about how Climate can create the right stimulus for motivation. This motivation provides an account for the management of the Change Equation. Recalling Festinger's (1957) Dissonance theory in Chapter 1 we can see the dynamic which needs to prevail if new behaviour is to both emerge and persist in order to achieve a sustainable change in behaviour and attitudes within organizations. The basic roadmap for achieving sustainable change is shown in Figure 3.3.

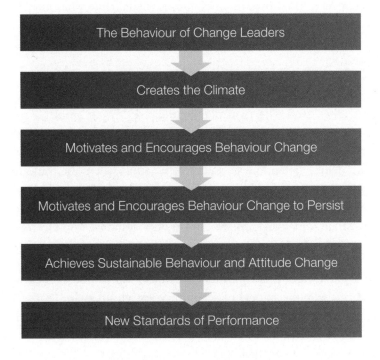

Figure 3.3. A time line for climate, behaviour and change

The behaviour of the change leader will create an effective Climate. This establishes the conditions for motivation followed by behavioural and eventually attitude change. The organization can now reap the benefits. However, it has taken time, effort and considerable energy to achieve this. We are now going to make this timeline of change even more detailed because in addition to the territory of dissonance, Climate and motivation, there is another theme of change psychology that we referred to in Chapter 1. This is the idea of individual differences in terms of character and personality theory. Or what we refer to as predisposition.

Predispositions: Individual Differences

It is self-evident that in some instances we are both similar to others and in some instances quite different. We can all think of colleagues who seem to enjoy thinking about the future and what might be, and yet there are other colleagues we can think of who prefer practical problem solving in terms of what needs to happen today. Similarly, we know people who like to talk and assert themselves and yet others who demonstrate more of a tendency to keep their own counsel and only challenge when they have to. This is sometimes referred to as "individual differences psychology" and is often positioned under the heading of personality traits. We prefer the term predisposition.

Rather than behaviour as such, we are referring to the idea of who and what you are, rather than what you may actually do. For example, a naturally reserved person may learn or adopt the behaviours of an outgoing person when the situation requires it (and vice versa). Similarly, a naturally cursory type can deliver attention to detail behaviour when the task requires exactitude and focused attention. However, neither of these individuals is likely to be able to sustain this "out of character" behaviour on a consistent basis nor when under pressure. So, by predisposition we are referring to the idea of an individual's set of natural preferences.

The understanding of predisposition, like that of motivation, is not in any way new and has been the subject of scientific research since the 1920s. As with motivation there is also a wide range of different frameworks. These include Raymond Cattell in the 1930s and 1940s (see Cattell 1946) and Costa and McRae in the 1970s and 1980s (see Costa and McCrae 1976 and McCrae and Costa 1987). Perhaps you have also been the recipient of feedback from a psychometric instrument such as the MBTI (Myers Briggs Type Indicator) or the OPQ (Occupational Personality Questionnaire) which also seek to understand our preferences to act in certain ways. The framework which we shall refer to in this narrative is the Global Predisposition Indicator or GPI™ (Glowinkowski 2012).

In the main, most of these frameworks are variations of the same theme. They endeavor to provide an individual profile of personality type or style. A kind of insight about an individual's natural style, preference or way of doing things. At the heart of the GPI™ framework are five fundamental predispositions (or traits) which are shown in Table 3.2.

INCREMENTAL	V	RADICAL
FOCUSED	V	FLEXIBLE
EXTROVERT	V	INTROVERT
COLLECTIVIST	V	INDIVIDUALIST
EXPRESSIVE	V	SELF CONTAINED

Table 3.2 Five Dimensions of Predisposition

An individual's predisposition has an enormous impact upon how they embrace and react with change. Focused individuals like to have change defined in a structured and detailed manner, whereas Flexible types prefer a less well structured approach. Extroverts are more likely to be vocal in their approach with Introverts less easy to read and perhaps more inclined to want to reflect on things on their own. Collectivists like to work in collegiate groups while an Individualist is more inclined to be a little detached and perhaps aloof. Finally, Expressive types are likely to act calmly and have lower self-esteem than Self-contained types.

Even from the brief description of predisposition above, we can understand the implications for the change leader in terms of how these predisposition styles may influence the change follower's reaction to change. This makes the management of the Change Equation very interesting indeed.

In Chapter 1 we introduced the concept of Incremental versus Radical thinking as that aspect of predisposition which is most closely associated with how individuals react to change. The concept of Incremental versus

Radical thinking was originally coined by Thurstone back in 1934. He used the idea of "closed versus open" to new ideas where individuals toward the closed end of the continuum are more predisposed to improve what already exists, i.e. they prefer to make things better. Individuals toward the open end of the continuum are wired to prefer to develop something new.

In Chapter 1 we talked about Incremental thinkers preferring to approach change a piece at a time, in small chunks as it were, where the practical next steps are clearly defined. Radical types on the other hand enjoy big and dramatic change, where a leap into the future is preferred. Often these different types look at each other pejoratively where Radicals are seen as unrealistic, risky and even mad. Incrementals on the other hand may be seen as boring, staid and essentially not willing to embrace the change.

As one might expect, all of these frameworks show a normal distribution across the metrics they measure. The idea of normal distribution is very important; from the world of nature and anthropology, it is a fundamental principle of measurement whether we are talking about height, eye color, leaf size or indeed intelligence. 67% of the population will rest one standard deviation either side of the mean. In other words, most people are "average." It is the minority whose natural styles lie at the extreme. George Bernard Shaw (1903) wrote: "The reasonable man adapts himself to the world: the unreasonable one persists in trying to adapt the world to himself. Therefore all progress depends on the unreasonable man." While we have found that such unreasonableness may cause change to occur, it tends not to be accepted willingly and therefore does not change attitudes unless it is managed with great care and thoughtfulness.

Personality and Behaviour – The Prism of Predisposition

Our research shows the following:

- By predisposition, i.e. underlying, stable, natural or preferred style, most change leaders tend to be Radical in their thinking style.

- Many change and strategy consultants are also very Radical in their thinking style.

- Employee groups are more typically distributed across the Incremental vs. Radical thinking style continuum, which the significant majority, some 67% of this population, will be one

60

standard deviation either side of the mean, i.e. hardly any will be extreme Radicals.

- Most change programs are articulated and defined in a Radical style and, furthermore, delivered by highly Radical people.

The fact that most change is developed and implemented by people at one end of a normal distribution is a rather sobering insight. It adds an additional level of complexity and thereby difficulty to implementing change successfully. It strengthens the reason why so much change fails to deliver projected benefits.

The clarion call from every book and article we review about change is that it must be done sooner, quicker, now! Change is all about "paradigm shifts" and tectonic movement. Change practice is governed by a number of renowned approaches and accompanying software that allow every minutiae to be planned and scheduled to evidence a clear "critical path" to implementation. While we would not dismiss this entirely out of hand, we do think it reflects a rather one-dimensional view in terms of considering the power of modern technology. And while technology has changed enormously, the actors, i.e. the people, have not changed one bit.

From the perspective of human psychology, whether we take into account being predispositionally Incremental or Radical, the ideas of motivation or Festinger's (1957) Dissonance theory, the bottom line for change is quite clear. It is a developmental process. Change is only ever going to happen in terms of most people coming on board in an incremental way where detail is provided to establish initial clarity of reason for the change, which is built upon through consistent and constant communication. Like a brick wall, understanding is built up row by row by row. This is not just our view but is underpinned by almost a century of research into human personality and motivation. Marketers may argue differently in terms of the speed at which social networking has exploded, the growth in digital download of music and other entertainment. That may be more due to the desire to interact with others and making life less complex, i.e. more Incremental than Radical, than the underlying trait style of thinking.

In 1934, Thurstone first identified the idea of five core personality variables of which the concept of thinking Incrementally or Radically was one. Motivation theory has a similar period of conception and gestation. For change leaders starting to "bang the drum" about the need to change, and their corralling of the failure to recognize and appreciate that the significant majority of people who will be affected by the change are much more Incremental, means the need to create a change Climate built upon the pillars of the Five Cs is paramount. For instance, while it may seem entirely practical to a Radical politician to introduce some "harder nosed" commercial practices into, say, higher education, they will fail to build Clarity and Commitment if they do not incrementalize and translate their language into the dialect the practitioners will understand. This is where Consistency and Constancy can bite back. Simply repeating the right message but in the wrong way will not win the hearts and minds of the 67% of the population who are not extreme Radical thinkers. And this attribute of thinking style is but one of many characteristic traits that form human personality, all of which show normal distribution.

The implication is that you can plan anything you like regarding your stage or set design, i.e. your strategy, but you still have to be patient and realistic when you deal with the actors. They are a temperamental bunch!

Looking back through history, there is no doubt that, in the broad sense, societies' beliefs, values and innate skills have changed, and mainly for the better, e.g. the unwinding of discriminatory attitudes toward race, religion, gender, sexual orientation and so on. But in terms of fundamental human personality and cognitive style it (as it has been defined by ourselves and numerous other researchers) has not changed one bit. In Elizabethan times, we almost certainly had our fair share of Extroverts and Introverts, those who were Optimistic or Pessimistic and, as we have concentrated upon in this chapter, those who think Incrementally or Radically.

It is important to recognize that the Incremental/Radical dimension is only one of the five. The other four dimensions will also impact massively on how the change followers perceive the communication and react to the change.

Thus, those change leaders who set out a strategy for their organization that necessitates some degree of change to occur need to learn to recognize and appreciate how all of their people, including their immediate colleagues and, indeed, themselves, are "wired." Such characteristics have a profound impact upon how their proposals and accompanying behaviours will be perceived. Put simply, one man's clarity is another's chaos; one person's friendliness is another's obsequiousness. In this sense, we should think of predispositions as the critical prism through which the behaviour of others, i.e. senior management, is perceived. The already complex process of change is made more knotty through having to consider the abstract convolutions of human nature. Figure 3.4 demonstrates the concept of the "prism of predisposition."

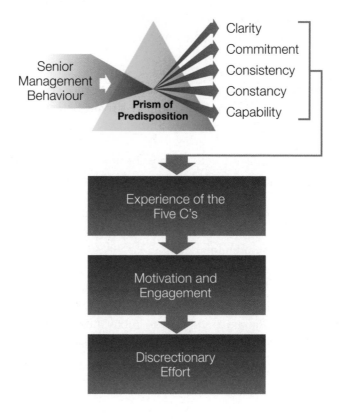

Figure 3.4: The Sequence and Prism of Predisposition

This model is designed to make you stop and think about whether, through your behaviours as a change leader, you are acting in a way that others, through the prism of their predispositions, will discern and experience a Climate in which they will devote additional discretionary effort. This is critical in order to bring through to successful conclusion the program of change that is required by the organization if it is to succeed in achieving its strategic aims.

Implicit in creating a Blue 4 culture is Self–awareness. The change leader needs to understand what underpins their own behaviour in terms of their predispositions. Also, how this style of behaviour impacts others. From the perspective of the change follower, developing insight about what drives them will also help them engage in the change process. Furthermore, Self-awareness will help facilitate the requirement of the Change Equation, i.e. the individual understanding the benefits of the change program to them and whether the pain of change is worth it.

Although beyond the scope of this book, much is written about Self–awareness; as an example, see Smith (2014). The model describes the reality of human nature as it affects what you are striving to lead your organization to accomplish.

We are not suggesting perfection is possible nor are we saying that given this complexity it is damn near impossible to achieve change unscathed.

Effective leadership is not defined by strategy formulation but rather by how effectively that strategy is executed. A necessary competency for an effective leader is to understand human nature.

This chapter has sought to accomplish one main objective: to describe the issues of individual human character and motivation. The first element was to link the Climate conditions to motivation in order to understand the dynamic relationship with the Change Equation and the realization of sustainable behavioural change. The second element was to reinforce the importance of predisposition in people's perception of change and its communication.

These dimensions need to be brought together in a harmonious yet stressed balance. Where that stress gets too severe, human nature is such that the desired Climate will not be experienced and, as a result, change will be impeded, potentially catastrophically. Change leaders require followers to succeed. "Follower" indicates willingness rather than coercion. People motivate themselves by being given by their leaders, through their behaviours, an environment in which they can flourish and utilize their full range of strengths and talents and, in so doing, develop and grow.

These first three chapters have mapped out the psychological reality of why change can be so difficult to achieve and, therefore, why most change programs fail to achieve their potential. Fundamental for the change leader is to establish the conditions for change to become sustainable. To achieve this they need to create a Climate of:

- **Clarity**
- **Commitment**
- **Consistency**
- **Constancy**
- **Capability**

These vital conditions enable change followers to feel motivated and for their individual predispositions to be accounted for in terms of their reaction to change. All of this enables people to feel engaged with the change process and thus establish sustainable behavioural and attitudinal change. It is the means by which change leaders can effectively manage the Change Equation.

The critical question is how can change leaders establish these Climate conditions for change – how do we do the Five Cs? In Chapter 1, we positioned the idea of Blue 4 behaviour as the route by which this can be achieved. Each of the next chapters is devoted to a particular aspect of Blue 4 behaviour. Each chapter provides a practical account of what needs to be done in order to create the type of Blue 4 culture which therefore enables the change leader to create the conditions for change.

CHAPTER 4

Strategy

Strategy, strategy, strategy – a term that has transfixed business leaders and academics alike. Business not performing well? Get a new strategy. Of course strategy is important – it is a key part of a leader setting direction, of being Blue 4. But we ask you to put it into perspective – you need a good strategy but, as importantly, you need great implementation. The importance of strategy is that it is the prerequisite for an organization to set direction and, as we showed in the Integrated Framework, Clarity is dependent upon an understanding of the direction of the enterprise. At its most simple (and effective) strategy is about how best to allocate scarce resources, about defining what the business is going to do and also what it is not going to do. Strategy is a prerequisite for business success but it is not sufficient in and of itself. Businesses need to have a strategy but they should not be preoccupied or obsessive about it. Rather their focus should be about putting strategy into action – in other words implement and, in this regard, we look to Blue 4 leadership as the prerequisite for success.

Perhaps you are now thinking that this has an inherent flaw because strategy must remain secret, locked away, only known to the privileged few who direct operations. Well, we would contend that this approach simply won't work because employees need to know and be engaged with the strategic context in which they work to avoid heading in the wrong direction. Certainly, some aspects of strategy – acquisition targets or divestment candidates or game changing new products - may need to be kept under lock and key but the strategy itself does not. Indeed, if you read most public company annual reports many set out clearly the company's strategy, albeit in a sanitized and PR-friendly form.

In our Introduction we talked about the importance of developing a carefully considered strategy as a prerequisite for developing a Climate that drives sustainable growth in the enterprise's value. Well, this is why the topic is so important. Failure to develop a well thought through strategy **and** to communicate it effectively **and** to fail to engage with employees on their role in delivery is a sure way to ensure a poor Climate and thus poor performance. Develop a great strategy and implement it effectively and business success will follow.

But first, it is worth reminding ourselves that strategy is ultimately about how the enterprise best allocates scarce resources (financial, human, reputational etc.) so as to be able to beat the competition and achieve a sustainable competitive advantage. Much has been written about how to "do" strategy but its essence is quite clear and, in some senses, quite commonplace: it concerns creating a plan of action to achieve a particular outcome over time. Tactics are how we implement our strategy. And both strategy and tactics are required to achieve success; as Sun Tzu (1910; 2002) said, "Strategy without tactics is the slowest route to victory. But tactics without strategy is simply the noise before battle."

While the Five Cs model as described in Chapter 2 is not concerned with strategy per se, it is very much concerned with tactics and represents a way of thinking about implementation that ensures all facets of change are properly considered.

To add to Sun Tzu, it is also important to avoid the trap of becoming too fixated or stuck in the strategizing phase – perhaps in part because this appears to be the intellectual or even "sexy" side of business. This is frustrating because strategy without action is an indulgence that adds no value whatsoever.

So, it is with this background that we want to reflect on how to think about strategy at both a practical and effective level. The frameworks that we use here are not ones that we have developed specifically for the purposes of this book. Instead they represent approaches that have been used successfully by strategy practitioners globally for many years. So there is no new news here - simply stuff that is tried and tested and has been found to be both practical and actionable. In short, what we are going to discuss is quite straightforward, and what's more it works!

A strategy is essential - whether we are talking about a manufacturing business, a financial services company, a school, a hospital or a charity - because it concerns how the organization's scarce resources are to best be deployed to achieve the organization's overall goals. For example, one school head that we know well described why her school was pursuing a certain academic specialism. The school was based in an economically and socially deprived community on the outskirts of a large city. "The pupils here are immersed in the celebrity culture, they want to win *The X Factor*." The school sought specialist qualification in arts and drama. It achieved this. The knock-on effect in subjects such as science and geography was considerable: science because it showed how the body functioned and needed nutrition to perform, and geography because it looked at countries from where themes for modern music genres had emerged.

In higher education, the need to take a longer, more considered view of what subjects to offer to market, the balance of tuition and research, the share of domestic and overseas customers (students), the quality and extent of pastoral provision are all now having to be much more actively reviewed as funding flows get squeezed. In this sense of value, these organizations are not so much assessing how to maximize shareholder return through growth of the bottom line but how best to utilize available funds to provide an educational experience that is valued and sought. In the charity sector, the recession has highlighted the need to look at how to run organizations more efficiently so that reduced donations are not swallowed up by unwieldy administration costs.

As this isn't a book about strategy, you may wish to read more widely on the topic and an extensive set of relevant references are listed at the end of the book. In our view, one of the clearest, most practical and enduring approaches to strategy formulation is that developed by Professor Michael Porter (1979; 1996; 2008) of Harvard Business School, probably the best known academic in his field. If you are interested in researching more about strategy then we recommend Porter's work as a first step. Inevitably, much that has followed since on the subject is essentially derivative; that is not to say that the approach of others can't be helpful or useful but it is because we have found Porter's approach to be so practical and accessible that we use it here. More recently, Richard Rumelt (2011) has written a compelling book *Good Strategy/Bad Strategy* and we also recommend this to you.

Strategy?

So, when we talk about strategy what exactly do we mean? At its simplest, strategy might be defined as the creation of a distinctive and value-creating competitive position carrying out a set of activities that are different from your competitors'. This means a company either performs different activities from its competitors or performs similar activities in different ways. Consider the airline industry:

- Emirates and British Airways are both full service airlines but Emirates flies via its hub in Dubai whereas BA flies most routes directly; so competing by doing things differently.

- Ryanair performs the same activity as British Airways, i.e. flying point-to-point but does it as a no-frills carrier rather than a full service airline. The activity is essentially the same but the manner in which it is delivered is very different.

Figure 4.1 below summarizes these differences.

What is Strategy?	
Strategy is...	**Strategy is not...**
• Creation of a unique and valuable position involving a differentiated set of activities By • Performing different activities to competitors Or • Performing similar activities in different ways	• Operational effectiveness • Strategic convergence • Productivity • Marketing • Benchmarking

Figure 4.1: What is Strategy?

Having been involved in strategy for many years as both recipients and architects, our view is that while developing a strategy is not in itself a particularly complicated process it does require careful planning, thoughtfulness and engagement. It also requires certain behavioural capabilities to augment the underlying techniques. It does not necessarily need external strategy consultants or even internal strategy departments, although we accept that there is a time and a place for everything. But, when external support is sought, an organization needs to guard against simply "outsourcing" its thinking to an external body. The danger being that it represents an abrogation of leadership responsibility that makes delivering on the Five Cs all the more challenging. Why? Because in many organizations the general belief is that the leadership doesn't really know what it is doing; calling in external consultants can exacerbate that belief. And as the clear role of a leader is to set direction, it is important that any direction is seen as belonging to that leader and their top team.

This can be further accentuated if only a few people at the top of the organization develop strategy. A strategy (and the associated change agenda) developed in the "corner office" without involving the organization's broader employee base is more liable to fail than one which is created through involvement and inclusion. But, as we said at the outset, isn't strategy by definition secret? In our view that certainly used to be the case but increasingly this view has proved to be unworkable. How can Clarity be created, how can an organization be Committed, how can systems and processes be made Consistent if the strategy is locked away in the corporate safe? Certainly, we are not advocating sharing M&A aspirations or detailed financial targets but we are advocating most strongly that the broad strategic direction and the key tactical levers be shared with all stakeholders.

Developing a strategy doesn't necessarily require huge leaps of imagination or creativity – the "Eureka" moment. What is does require is the mindfulness to search patiently for the insights that will enable the organization to distinguish itself from its peers so it becomes more profitable or financially efficient – perhaps the "Aha" moment!

Insight is a key concept in the development of a good strategy. It embraces both technical skill and appropriate behavioural adeptness. Insight represents a higher level of understanding about your organization's industry or market sector. It concerns acquiring and maintaining astute knowledge of the dynamics at play, be they political, economic, social, or technological. It also concerns knowing one's competitors and, crucially, potential competitors. How might other organizations move up and down their respective value chains to enter your market? How, through acquisition, might a highly successful player in another market become a ferocious competitor in your market?

Insight enables an organization to calibrate itself against its peers and determine the extent of any competitive advantage it may possess. Insight does not restrict itself to the here and now but should provide the means by which an organization can determine what may lie beyond the horizon. The greater the complexity, the further out insight needs to stretch, anticipating future dynamics and changes that may harm or benefit the organization's competitive position within its industry or, indeed, the industry itself.

But insight alone is not enough; often quite successful companies fail because they don't anticipate or respond to changes in their competitive environment. Often new entrants to a market with a new model are, at the outset, less profitable than the incumbent companies and so there is little incentive for the incumbents to respond. However, the new entrant has a great incentive to claw its way to greater efficiency and profitability and once they have succeeded then they may well have turned the tables on the incumbents.

For example, Sony "invented" the portable music player with the Walkman but Apple annihilated them with the iPod and iTunes.

Businesses need to adapt or die even if they need to embrace what initially looks like a less profitable business model. Clayton Christensen (1997) dubbed this the "innovator's dilemma" referring to the need to respond to the initially less efficient and profitable new entrant who has no existing business to defend. Jack Welch at GE talked about the need to think about how to destroy your existing business and to actually do so if the alternative scenario was compelling enough in the longer term (Lowe 1998). John Lewis, an upmarket UK multiple retailer with high street and out-of-town locations, has embraced the internet and added a feature that internet-only companies can't compete with: you can order online but collect from a store, usually the next day. The convenience of shopping at home, faster delivery and no need to wait home for your goods to arrive. Neat, right?

Having spent years developing strategy in some shape or form we were tempted to simply dive into a quick primer of how to do it but over time we have also learned that there are a few guiding principles that are pretty important. These principles are the ones that have worked best for us and are designed to help you decide how to approach the subject and they need to be discussed internally before the strategy process commences.

The Guiding Principles of Formulating Strategy

1. Challenge *all* your assumptions

A key to gaining insight is to challenge the assumptions or sacred cows that pertain about the industry or company. Try these questions:

a. *How do the best players in your industry make money? Or in the noncommercial sector how do they utilize their funding?*

Consider the mining business. It is big and complex. However, the essence of making money is to have very high quality, low-cost, long-life assets in commodity sectors, e.g. coal, iron ore, bauxite, that will experience strong supply/demand fundamentals. Essentially in mining this means being at the bottom end of the industry cost curve, i.e. being strongly efficient and productive in utilization of underlying capital (financial, physical and human) in products that China and India consume in huge quantities but which they don't mine in sufficient volumes themselves to affect either supply or the marginal price.

Having high-cost assets in high-demand products isn't good. If prices fall, you will be very exposed to losses if you sit at the top of the cost curve. Equally, being at the bottom end of the cost curve in commodities in which China is self-sufficient largely rules out demand-induced price inflation.

This is why it is absolutely fundamental for a business to understand precisely how the company makes its money: what is the essence of the end-to-end business process? But what about this insight issue? Well, knowing how you make money is a pretty good starting point but that alone isn't going to be enough.

b. *What is it that distinguishes the best performers from the worst?*

Do you really understand why you outperform your competitors or vice versa? Why do investors rate your competitors ahead of you or vice versa?

These things don't happen by chance; over time customers and markets are pretty rational and unsentimental.

Who in your business has the best products, best distribution, best geographical spread, best production costs, best people, best innovation, best reputation, best growth rates? However painful, it is vital to understand what distinguishes the top achievers from the also-rans. And if you are the "best" then you had better think hard about which of the attributes that separate you from your competitors is really distinctive, differentiating and really sustainable.

Reverting to the natural resources industry there are three key insights:

- First, participate in the most attractive commodities, e.g. copper and iron ore

- Second, participate in the most profitable part of the value chain – typically the upstream part

- Third, own the best assets: low cost, long life, stable geographies

Importantly, in the main, each of these three attributes is controllable by the industry participant. Thus, while a firm cannot influence commodity demand or exchange rates to any material degree, it can choose which commodities, where in the value chain and which resources it chooses to develop.

Lastly, challenging one's assumptions rigorously guards against the lessons of history, i.e. "We tried this before and it failed"; guards against negative thinking, i.e. "We would never be allowed to do that"; and guards against acting in an inferior manner, i.e. "We don't have the capability."

While all of these may be legitimate concerns, it could also be that things failed before because of ineffective implementation. It is always worth asking what you would need to do to be allowed to do something or how you would acquire the capability to enact something. Many great strategies come from people who are prepared to challenge the tried and tested path, or to challenge convention. Be prepared to interrogate your beliefs, prejudices and assumptions before allowing them to shape your strategy. If not, you risk producing the "emperor's new clothes" and in such cases it is then the market that identifies your constraints, which is too late and will, at best, be damaging financially; at worst, it could be catastrophic.

2. Think broadly

Senior leaders need to appreciate and understand their own organization from the origins of its supply chain to the ongoing management and maintenance of clients and customers. They need to understand their industry or market sector. They also need to be curious about the world around them. The most successful strategists we have met are "citizens of the world" and are hugely curious and open-minded. They are concerned with "why" things happen as they do and what could disturb the apparent equilibrium. They understand the "innovator's dilemma." This requires people to read broadly and engage widely with people within and beyond one's industry. This networking or relationship management is vitally important, so much so that we devote a large part of Chapter 9 to the topic.

Thus, as you begin the strategy process you need to be able to map those major external influences on your industry and business we mentioned earlier, i.e. the PEST factors, and how these might affect positively or negatively the future of the firm. Behaviourally, we are talking about the leadership qualities of Conceptual Thinking, and Broad Scanning, or indeed, seeing the bigger picture (see Chapter 6).

3. Look ahead

Strategy is rarely concerned with the here and now. More often it is concerned with positioning a company to either make something happen or to take advantage of something that might happen. Great leaders don't watch things happen, or wonder what happened, they make things happen and the same might well be said about great strategists.

4. Question incisively

Much that can be regarded as insight is derived from asking carefully constructed but challenging questions such as:

    a. How do we make money in this business?

    b. Why are our competitors better than us?

    c. What do our customers really need and want? What will they no longer want?

   d. What could derail our ambitions?

   e. What are the longer term dynamics of supply and demand?

   f. How could our product/service become obsolete?

   g. How good are our people? How can we make them better?

The use of such open-ended questions contributes significantly to the process of challenging assumptions by demanding both breadth of thinking as well as more analytical or forensic analysis. The questions do not in themselves contain any hint of the answer.

Behaviourally, we are talking about the leadership qualities of Analytical Thinking, Forward Thinking, Critical Information Seeking and Strategic Thinking (Chapter 6).

5. Be inclusive

While there is an element of confidentiality involved in the formulation of strategy it is of paramount importance to involve enough people of differing views and experience to ensure that the strategy discussion is rich, diverse and comprehensive. There is no point developing a strategy if one excludes people who are able to bring critical knowledge or insight. To do so risks not only having a poorly formulated strategy but failing to win the Commitment and build the Clarity required for effective implementation.

Most people respect being included in the strategy process and find it very motivating. They understand the need for confidentiality and rarely breach this requirement. If there is a leak we would advise looking upward rather than downward in the organization – the most senior are usually the loosest lipped!

6. Be time bound

Strategy processes can become quite protracted and this can turn into a huge downside as the company falls into "paralysis by analysis." So being curious and inquiring is good but perfect knowledge or information is not attainable so one must equally know when to stop. Imposing a fixed deadline by which the strategic analysis and interpretation must be completed, including some intermediary checkpoints to ensure progress is being made, is effective in focusing minds, winning attention and galvanizing action.

7. Resource the process

While developing strategy doesn't require huge numbers of people, it does require a minimum of resource to run the process, conduct background analysis and prepare associated reports.

In a divisional structure, a minimum of three or four people would be required for a reasonably serious process, e.g. a head of strategy or planning director who is clearly seen as the leader of the process and accountable for it being undertaken efficiently and effectively. That person will need a couple of support analysts.

Much of the big analytical workload takes place in the business units and therefore they require a parallel structure as well. This is the structural arrangements experience of the authors during their respective careers.

8. Keep it simple

A common refrain is "This business is really complicated." Is that necessarily so or are certain organizational leaders just too stupid or idle to really understand their enterprise? In a recent interview in the UK's *Sunday Times*, Cameron Clyne, CEO of National Australia Bank remarked, "They [Boeing] take something like 6m parts from 400 suppliers in 40 countries and in 11 days turn it into a 747. That is complexity. In some banking organizations they can't even get a credit card statement and a savings account statement in the same envelope." (Ashton 2009)

In recognizing that the external business environment is invariably complicated, things can be made easier by identifying which variables you do not and will not be able to control and accepting these as such. This enables focus, drive and energy to be applied to the factors over which you do have some degree of control, e.g. pace of R&D in consumer electronics to deliver new and enhanced products to market.

And consider this: if the business is so complicated that it is difficult to explain, how can you hope to convince shareholders and employees that you know what you are talking about?

These eight guiding principles provide the ground rules for the process of formulating strategy. Let us now consider some practical techniques to use within the process.

The overall process for setting strategic direction

The process for developing strategy or setting strategic direction can be thought of in four distinct stages as set out in Figure 4.2.

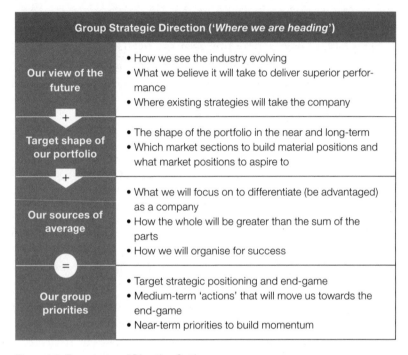

Figure 4.2: Four stages of Direction Setting

To re-affirm what we said at the beginning of this book, this process does have a preliminary stage in terms of really knowing your business - assumption is a dangerous friend. "Knowing" demands evidence. "Knowing" demands a fact base, and a foundation activity of good strategy development is often the development of a comprehensive fact base. Accepting that such a fact base has been prepared, the first stage is developing a clear view of the future: how is the industry likely to evolve, where do we see the business heading within that evolutionary context and what will be required to deliver superior performance in terms of assets and activity?

Secondly, we need to ensure that we are clear about what the future portfolio should look like: what do we want more of or less of, and what do we think our natural market position should be?

Thirdly, we need to be clear on our sources of competitive advantage: what is going to differentiate us, how does it all fit together and how will we organize for success?

And finally, what therefore are our (i.e. the leadership team's) critical few priorities in both the near-term and in the medium-term? Critical – those that are truly mission critical. Few – because we have scarce resources and we have to deploy them on the biggest impact items only (five maximum).

Stage one: Our view of the future

Industry analysis

Key to developing your view of the future are two linked pieces of analysis:

- Are you in an industry or market that is favorable compared to others in which you could compete?

- Within that industry or market, do you have or can you develop a competitive position that is more advantaged than your competitor peer group?

We know that it is possible to develop a fantastic business in a poor industry - usually by operating in a niche of some kind - but for the sake of simplicity let's stay with the prime premise. Focus on being in attractive markets in which you can create an advantaged position.

Analyzing your industry/markets

Thinking in terms of a market is important because it begins to establish the boundaries within which you operate. It is important to define these boundaries carefully as broad or vague definitions rarely help. Precision is required because one of the first things you need to decide is whether the industry in which you operate is structurally attractive or not. For example, if you are manufacturing and selling paint to domestic consumers are you involved in the coatings industry, the paint industry, or the decorative paint industry? If one chooses either of the first two it is difficult to reach a satisfactory conclusion on whether the industry is fundamentally a good one or not. Metal packaging coatings may be a lousy business, automotive OEM coatings may be similar, automotive re-finish a bit better, but decorative coatings may be pretty good. So a failure to be precise may lead one to conclude, erroneously, that as a decorative paint manufacturer you operate in a lousy industry when in fact the opposite is true. Similarly with a service business looking at entering a new sector - for instance, the power sector. This is simply too wide to analyse constructively: does it relate to power generation or transmission, does it mean nuclear, coal or "green", does it mean construction of reactor halls or maintenance of office suites? The "industry" needs to be bounded in a balanced and definable manner, i.e. neither too extensive nor too narrow. Over time, experienced strategists gain an intuitive sense of what feels right.

Market analysis requires one to understand the nature of the markets to the extent that one can conclude whether it has a structure that enables those who operate within it to make a reasonable return on their investment. Michael Porter, to whom we referred earlier, conducted this analysis on the basis of five forces:

- The relative power of suppliers

- The relative power of customers

- The likelihood of substitution for the product or service

- The ease by which new participants can enter the industry (or, conversely, the ease by which participants can leave it)

- The degree of rivalry among competitors

Clearly, if suppliers and customers have power, substitution is easy, it is easy to enter the industry and there are a lot of competitors, then it is unlikely that this will be a place where people make much money.

If the reverse is true then the likelihood of making good money is correspondingly higher. Naturally, reality is often far more complicated than that but hopefully the point is clear.

Most other takes on strategy essentially make very similar points. Having a framework such as the five forces is helpful because it provides a frame of reference and lends discipline to the thinking process and so builds evidential understanding.

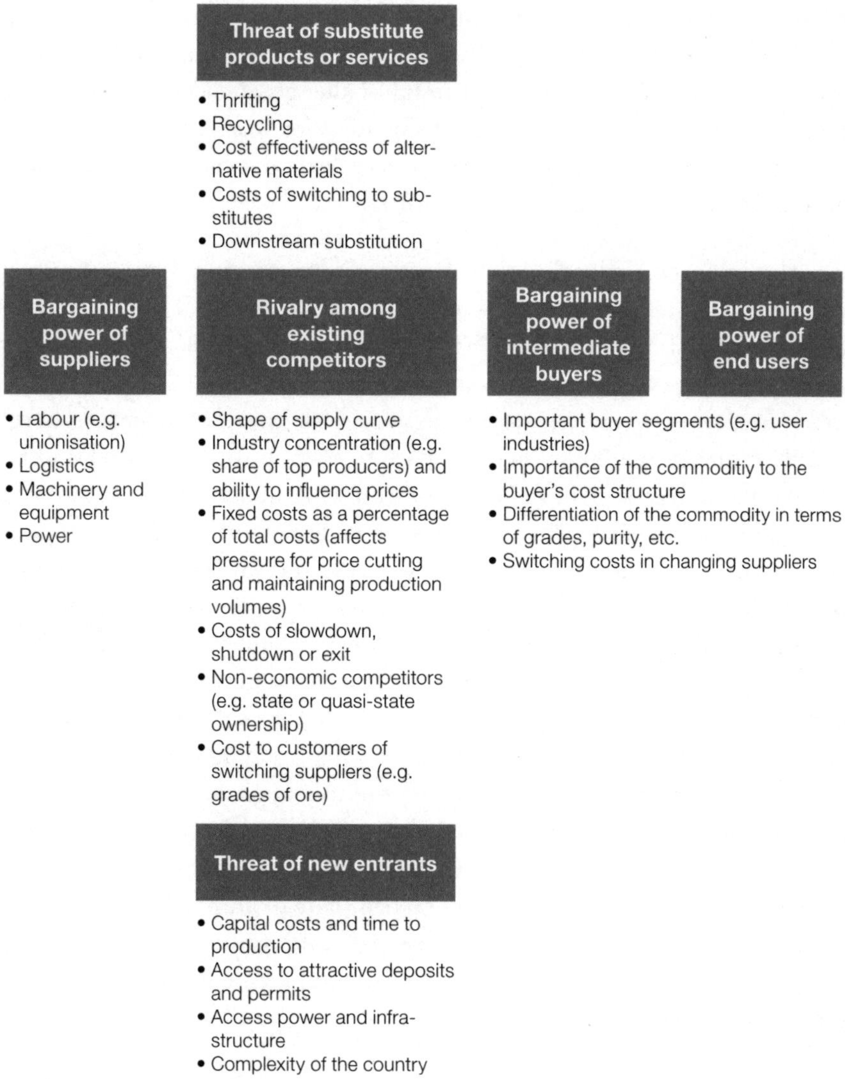

Threat of substitute products or services

- Thrifting
- Recycling
- Cost effectiveness of alternative materials
- Costs of switching to substitutes
- Downstream substitution

Bargaining power of suppliers

- Labour (e.g. unionisation)
- Logistics
- Machinery and equipment
- Power

Rivalry among existing competitors

- Shape of supply curve
- Industry concentration (e.g. share of top producers) and ability to influence prices
- Fixed costs as a percentage of total costs (affects pressure for price cutting and maintaining production volumes)
- Costs of slowdown, shutdown or exit
- Non-economic competitors (e.g. state or quasi-state ownership)
- Cost to customers of switching suppliers (e.g. grades of ore)

Bargaining power of intermediate buyers

Bargaining power of end users

- Important buyer segments (e.g. user industries)
- Importance of the commoditiy to the buyer's cost structure
- Differentiation of the commodity in terms of grades, purity, etc.
- Switching costs in changing suppliers

Threat of new entrants

- Capital costs and time to production
- Access to attractive deposits and permits
- Access power and infrastructure
- Complexity of the country

Figure 4.3: Industry Structure in Mining Industries

Analyzing your position within your industry

The next step is to take a look at how your business is positioned within the industry analyzed (Figure 4.3 above). This stage requires complete honesty and care, for it is at this stage that it is easy to delude oneself or ignore or rationalize away uncomfortable facts. Beware of selective data selection and always guard against that which you most want to be true.

Strategy is an iterative and thoughtful process. It is rarely one in which there is a huge leap of thinking and rarely does it happen through individual brilliance. Instead, a process of careful challenge and debate among the senior leadership team, some external advisors where appropriate, and involvement of internal colleagues is required to generate the required insight that leads to genuine strategic progress.

It is also important to realize that the strategy process is designed simply to ensure that scarce resources are allocated appropriately. Thus, it is about making choice between competing interests and demands and therefore it is not a process in which everyone can have his or her demands met. In this sense, strategy involves an element of risk because effective strategy usually requires treading a different path to one's competitors. In choosing this path it is necessary to reflect deeply on what qualities or competencies the company possesses that enables such differentiation. The concept of core competencies at the level of the organization was originally developed by Prahlad and Hammel (1990): "*Core competence of the corporation*, Harvard Business Review (v68 no3) pp. 79-91." A core competence is an attribute that the company possesses which is difficult for competitors to imitate, is applicable across the product range and which adds value to the consumer, client or customer. A competence that meets these definitions is one on which it would make sense to build a strategy primarily because it creates a barrier to entry. Such a competence is likely to be either a piece of technology, a cultural attribute or specialist knowledge or relationships. So, while Honda's product range is very broad, i.e. hedge trimmers to automobiles, it is based upon its core competence with the internal combustion engine. Businesses that have intentionally or unintentionally diluted their core competence lose their competitiveness.

Strategy is also about differentiating the enterprise from others operating in the same or similar industry. It is not about copying a competitor. It is not about all organizations looking the same. Richard Branson started his airline Virgin Atlantic by remarking, "We are in the entertainment business, albeit at 35,000 feet!" In this there is, therefore, an inherent risk for the market leader because making choices involves risk. The risk can be minimized by the quality of the strategic thinking process but it cannot, because perfect information can never exist, ever be eradicated. Perhaps this is why some organizations strategically decide to be "second-movers" by building the capability to replicate success quickly once it has been proven.

Stage Two: Target shape of the portfolio

Having carried out the first stage, which pieces of the current portfolio do you need to develop, which pieces do you need to exit and are there pieces that you need to acquire? Very often this consideration relates to extending activity up and/or down a product's or service's value chain.

A UK coatings company that operated in OEM automotive paint, re-finish automotive paint and decorative paint determined to exit from the first two and to focus on just decorative paint. However, within that category opportunities were identified and subsequently realized by adding painting accessories and wood stains to the portfolio and stretching the geographic reach of the business significantly beyond the home base.

Stage Three: Determining sources of competitive advantage

In the paint company mentioned, it was determined that it possessed three key differentiators:

- That its products actually worked because of great R&D
- That consumers loved its products because of great marketing
- That retailers loved stocking it because of outstanding customer service

Therefore, resources were focused on further building these capabilities and extending their application into new product areas. Equally as important as the decisions about what would be done were those about what would not be done, which were:

- Not to focus on excellent, low-cost but inflexible production processes
- Not to cut advertising spend to boost short-term profitability
- Not to cut the in-store salesforce

Stage Four: Setting the group's priorities and, thereby, the leadership team's direction

The paint company then discussed with its board that it would focus on decorative paint only, that it would invest more money in state-of-the-art research facilities, that it would acquire adjacent companies where it could add value and it would always use consumer satisfaction metrics as well as short-term financial measures as a way of measuring whether or not it was building on its core competencies.

Stage Five: Implementation planning

It is vital not to stop at developing strategy – that is, generally, the easy part. In addition one needs to pull the thinking together with a clear and achievable plan. A good start point is the Strategy Diamond developed by Hambrick and Fredrickson (2001).

As seen in Figure 4.4 below it has five elements:

- Arenas – Where will we be active (and with what emphasis)?
- Vehicles – How will we get there?
- Differentiators – How will we win?
- Staging – What is the speed and sequence of delivery?
- Economic Logic – How will we obtain our returns?

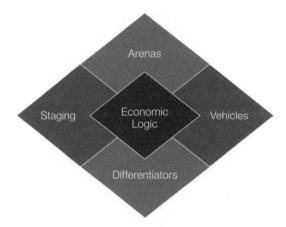

Figure 4.4: The Strategy Diamond

The Strategy Diamond is very useful for summarizing the strategic thinking, testing its validity, summarizing the implementation plan and, importantly, creating a simple and practical test for commercial viability.

The Rhythm of Strategy

Strategy is necessarily an evolving and ongoing process. Often it is regarded as an annual process and often consumes a disproportionate amount of time and effort. Unless there are major structural changes in an industry we do NOT regard it as necessary that the process be run in full every year. Instead, a process that sets out a three- or five-year strategy that is reviewed annually for appropriateness and completeness is all that is required.

Conclusion

We worry over strategy for two reasons. Firstly, without a clear and differentiated strategy, business success is simply a matter of chance – and surely your stakeholders have a right to expect more? Secondly, that without strategy it is impossible to attain one of the critical elements of being a Blue 4 leader: a clear and well-communicated sense of direction. Sure, having a strategy doesn't necessarily mean that one will succeed in communicating direction effectively but without a strategy you will surely fail. To be truly effective, business leaders then need to focus on the change process which implements the strategy.

CHAPTER 5

Agenda

We all know that change is a journey but we are amazed that organizations often set out without a fully formed idea of where they are going and why. And while a well thought through strategy will create a compelling rationale and way forward, there is a bit more preparation required before jumping into the change program. If strategy is about defining the What then understanding the size of the change gap is very much about beginning to define the How.

So assessing the gap is all about defining, before heading out on the journey from whence you are starting, where you want to go to, how far it is and how long it will take. And so, in this chapter, we will introduce you to the tools required to plan a change journey fully and well.

The Change Equation

At the start of the book we referred to the Change Equation as one of the foundations of change management and it is an extremely useful diagnostic tool in the journey planning phase. As you will recall, the equation has three key components:

1. **Dissatisfaction** – are people so dissatisfied with the way things are currently that they are motivated to go through the pain and inconvenience of changing?

2. **Future-state/vision** – is there a clear vision of the end destination that is well articulated and compelling enough that people feel it is a worthwhile goal?

3. **First steps** – given that the future-state may represent a huge leap forward, are there some early wins that can get people started on the road to the future-state, i.e. chunking up the elephant into bite-sized pieces that make the overall challenge less daunting or ensuring that there are some quick wins so momentum builds early on in the process?

However, while very useful, the Change Equation isn't very explicit in the requirement to have a good understanding of the current state or the way things are now. In our view, conducting this analysis is a crucial part of the process, not least because it helps establish two of the Five Cs: Clarity and thus Commitment. Quite simply, it isn't good enough to have a general view of the current state or for it to be implied because it is quite likely that different members of the team will have a different view on exactly what things are like at the present time. Analogously, it is similar to everyone agreeing to visit London. The team knows it is traveling from Scotland and each individual is enthusiastic about the journey. However, one person thinks she is in John O'Groats, another believes that he is in Glasgow and another is convinced that she is on the Isle of Mull. In fact they are all in Edinburgh! Now if each has their location, or view of the current situation, as an implicit assumption, each will plan a different journey and none of them will start off on the correct road.

This is why defining where you are or the current state is so important.

Gap Analysis

In defining the current state a few simple rules are required. The rules are so simple and obvious that we considered omitting them until we recalled the number of people who overlooked these basic points. In many ways the devil is in the detail at this point and generalizations aren't much help. Just as with doing strategy, some principles are helpful and we have found very much to be required in defining the gap. There are only three of them which we set out briefly below and then expand upon subsequently. As with all of the principles that we have developed over the years, these are all both necessary and sufficient.

1. Be honest

Getting a precise measure of the change required is important and, therefore, all members of the management team must be engaged in the process and their honest views obtained and evaluated. This is not the time for being less than absolutely candid about how things really are! It isn't that people are dishonest, it is just that they may not say what they think. Why? Well it could be that they are afraid of upsetting the boss or another powerful team member, that they are rather introverted and thus won't proffer a view until asked, or they simply find expressing any view that might be seen as dissenting as extremely difficult.

So to gain honesty in the process, the leader has not only to give express permission but also behave accordingly, perhaps even expressing a controversial view themselves. Also consider one-on-one discussion not just group meetings. In fact, ensure that everyone is heard and has the opportunity to be heard in the way they find most comfortable.

2. Be specific about weaknesses

In discussions, ensure the terms being used by individuals are understood to mean the same thing; for instance, "being insufficiently commercial" is a phrase that hides a multitude of sins. What does the individual actually mean? What specific evidence do they have for indicating, say, that they consider their enterprise is not actually a meritocracy? Being specific is also linked with being honest and once again the leader needs to ensure that people really explain in some detail precisely what they mean – to explain their point of view rather than justify. So, being "insufficiently commercial" might mean that the business always sets its prices too high or low, or has an inadequately staffed or trained salesforce, has poor distribution channels, or all of the above! So spell it out each and every time or a simple phrase could be interpreted differently by everybody in the room.

3. Be precise about improvements

Just as one needs to be specific about deficiencies one also needs precision as to objectives. So "being more effective commercially" is a worthless type of objective but "increasing salesperson call and cold call rates by 20%" is nice and specific and measurable. So we would expect that for every honest statement of deficiency there is a precise statement of objective that is clear and measurable – or even better, SSMART: Stretching, Specific, Measurable, Achievable, Relevant and Timebound.

But what about the gap?

So, with these rules as the foundation for any discussion concerning constructing a map of current-state, there are then two subsequent steps that we need to take. Perhaps like the rules or principles that we discussed above they seem rather obvious but, as we know, the fact that it is obvious doesn't mean that it is actually implemented. So these two steps are vital parts of making things happen:

    a. Define the gap between current-state and desired future-state

    b. Develop a detailed "roadmap" (or plan) of how you are going to complete the journey from current-state to future-state

Let us take each in turn.

Step One: Gap assessment

    i. Develop a From/To Chart

This is a relatively straightforward process but begins to create significant momentum as the team begins to commit to paper and begins to put detail around both their definition of the problem and their view of the solution.

- Accurately define where you are now and where you want to be
- Avoid group think during the process

To help with the honesty issue, we suggest that each member of the team is asked to produce their own version of this chart independently and then to share it with their colleagues in a team meeting; in doing so remembering that whatever they write must also be specific and precise as we defined earlier. The only downside of requiring individual work is the requirement to subsequently synthesize into a final product but the benefits of acting this way vastly outweigh this particular downside.

An example of an output arising from one factor is given below in Figure 5.1.

Assessing the Gap	
From...	**To...**
• Production focused	**• Customer focused**
Our production facilities are very efficient but inflexible. We deliver to customers when we have produced it rather than when they need it.	We will ask our customers when they need it and do our upmost to deliver. We will make production more flexible and will happily bear the extra cost that this entails.
Our customer service staff are essentially involved in applying rigid rules and trying to stop the customer getting too upset when they don't get what they want when they need it.	We will give our customer service staff both the training and the freedom to act (within limits) to delight the customer.
Our delivery drivers are famed for being rude and inflexible. They never tell people when they are going to turn up. Without warning some of our customers are simply unprepared for their delivery.	Our delivery drivers will be trained and rewarded for the quality of their customer interaction. They will call the customer a couple of hours before they are going to turn up.

Figure 5.1: Assessing the Gap

ii. Once the From/To chart is developed then the time has arrived to describe in detail precisely what is required to close the gap between the From and To states.

- In doing this it is important to consider carefully the consequences of making the change.

  For example, a move to more flexible production will require a different production planning process where the sales teams and the production team talk with each other and take some joint responsibility for sales forecasting and production planning.

  Such flexibility could well lead to production costs per unit that are higher than currently is the case. So at this point the team needs to decide whether this is really what they meant when they decided to move from one state to another. Will they get the commercial benefit required?

If it isn't – say that people really meant "we are going to be much more flexible AND drive down unit production costs" – ask if this is actually practical and realistic and then work on exactly how this would happen. It is very important to really thrash out all the detail and all the consequences before committing to action. Of course, it's frustrating but it ensures that no avenue is left unexplored and also that the organization doesn't commit to something with unimagined or unintended consequences.

Step Two: Develop the roadmap

i. Using the gap analysis data

The team now needs to formulate a map of the actions that need to take place to get the change program moving.

In the first phase, a key activity relates to validating the views captured during the first step. Validation is critical because the team needs to ensure that they have enough understanding of the detail to ensure what they are proposing is both practical and actionable. It is at this point that some consultation with subject matter experts either from within the business or from outside is required. Consultation as a carefully planned way with others in the organization has two benefits. Obviously, it utilizes existing internal knowledge but it also contributes to building support down the organization.

It is easy to conjecture that a top team should know about these things but, depending on the size of the business, this is not necessarily the case. Even if the senior leaders consider they have their finger on the pulse, consulting with those employees whose direct accountability concerns such issues at this early stage helps build Commitment. False starts can be avoided, which are damaging to any change initiative. Obvious risks are more likely to be identified and mitigated against as well.

In our experience, this stage of detailed scrutiny is often overlooked in a fit of enthusiasm to "just do it." "Fire, ready, aim" can be the accusation leveled at the leadership team. Clearly that wasn't their intent (most leadership teams aren't willfully stupid) but it does occur because they thought they knew all they needed to know when in fact some wider consultation may have saved them from a few pitfalls and subsequent fine-tuning. It is not that we are necessarily advocating going slowly for the sake of it but rather that taking the time at the start of the project to be absolutely thorough and detailed will ensure that subsequent progress is both quicker and more effective. Often this is referred to as "front end loading."

Thinking ahead, anticipation, asking "what if": all change initiatives progress more quickly if fully incorporated at the planning stage. Remember that no business operates in a vacuum and thus thinking through customer, competitor and stakeholder responses is a key part of getting the planning right. You need sufficient detail to ensure Clarity but you also need enough agility and flexibility to adapt to the conditions that you encounter en-route. As when using a Satnav, initially the route is "zoomed out" until nearing the destination and you can "zoom in" to pin-point your specific destination. In this way, a major change initiative can be steered around the many potential pitfalls it will encounter during its tenure of existence. This is a neat trick to pull off.

ii. Who's driving, who's navigating, when do we arrive?

Producing the roadmap doesn't just concern defining the direction to be taken and initial actions. It also encompasses defining who is accountable for specific activities and all of them collectively. It is essential that someone is put in place who is clearly responsible for getting things going and who is supported by a team that is appropriate for the task. Their tenure, objectives and reporting line needs to be spelt out clearly. And whatever the people are called and however they are organized it is essential that they have the complete and public backing from the boss.

Because while we devote a subsequent chapter to stakeholder management and the application of influencing behaviours, at its most cynical it remains a fact of organizational life that sometimes a bit of positional power is required to overcome organizational inertia. At its most constructive, great leaders stand up and support their people and don't duck or hide from tackling difficult issues of the sort that always occur when change happens. That doesn't mean to say the boss has to make every pronouncement, attend every meeting or sign every edict but they do have to be sure that they are seen as personally and publically supporting the change program and whoever is the change leader.

Naturally, setting milestones is vitally important. These can be more accurately determined through taking an inclusive approach during this initial stage as, if honesty does prevail, the front-line operators are able to tell the difficulties likely to be encountered along the way. They know where a small change made to a process can produce exponentially bigger ramifications, e.g. changing timing of inbound logistics of different components sees everything arrive at once, and with insufficient storage, capacity inventory is damaged and cost of production escalates.

The big danger is that any change process starts off with a huge amount of effort and energy but then subsequently loses momentum. Often this is because one of the Five Cs has been neglected. There isn't enough Clarity, the Commitment of the top team isn't really there, their systems and processes of the organization are not Consistent with the change desired, Constancy is lost as the top team become distracted by other events or declare victory too early, or somehow or other the organization or the change team itself lacks the Capability or resources to deliver on the project plan.

In such a case it is easy for things to lose momentum and for people to become demoralized. Having milestones that are clear and regularly reviewed by the top team will enable problems to be spotted quickly and corrective actions to be put in place. When conducting acquisitions, one of the authors made sure that the post-acquisition plan was absolutely nailed down before the acquisition was made. He then had weekly reviews of the milestones until he was satisfied that things were headed in the right direction when the frequency was reduced to monthly and eventually quarterly until all the actions were completed and synergies gained.

So, in a major transitional change that may last 18 months or more, initially the roadmap's "scale" should show a detailed project plan for, say, up to six months and a less detailed timeline beyond that. In these first weeks and months, the senior team, particularly the individual from that team who has "sponsored" the initiative, needs to review and evaluate progress but without appearing not to distrust or undermine the judgment of the person they have appointed to manage the program and made accountable for so doing. Such review must be positioned in a supportive manner not a managing manner. Quite often, some additional resource may be required to crack a particular obstacle that has been encountered not so much by surprise but more by its extent or difficulty to resolve.

Once everyone is satisfied that the journey is well underway and a good head of steam has been built up, the review frequency can be reduced. However, we find that ongoing intervention by the senior team can help pre-emptive reshaping of planned activity through their ongoing broad scanning of the external environment. However, this is no excuse for presumptive and impulsive scope creep, the most fatal disease that can strike any change initiative. Figure 5.2 summarizes what happens.

Gap definition questions	Key issues	Links to the 5 Cs
Why?	Why are we seeking to change? • Define the rationale in detail with clear outcome statements – the case for change	CLARITY
What?	What are the expected benefits? • The Return for our Change investment	COMMITMENT
Who?	Who is leading the Change programme and associated processes? • Who is Responsible? • Who is Accountable? • Who is involved • What are the Resources allocated?	CAPABILITY
When?	Timescale for delivery • In detail • With Milestones	CONSTANCY
How?	Acceptable methods of approach/delivery • Issues and sensitivities • Ensuring that all aspects fit together	CONSISTENCY

Figure 5.2: Defining the Gap

If you wish, the "why" is the business case and projected return on investment (ROI) or demonstration that the venture clears internal rate of return (IRR) hurdles.

In this chapter we have covered some simple but effective ways to plan the change journey. In the following chapters we also introduce the concept of Influencing as a key component for change success. As part of the Influencing model we use a simple but effective nine-box model (Chapter 9) and this approach can also be used to aid the change planning process. You may prefer the techniques that we describe here or you may prefer to adapt the model we describe later – and you should use whichever works for you. Just make sure that you don't skip the step entirely.

Case Studies

These case studies are taken from real life examples but have been modified to protect confidentiality. We hope that they begin to bring what has gone before to life and will stimulate some thinking and reflection.

Case 1: Improving Safety Performance

A large multinational, multidivisional industrial company set out to improve its global safety performance. Now this is a complex challenge because of the multifaceted nature of the business and the fact that safety actually happens at both an organizational (in terms of establishing the Climate) and individual (in terms of behaving safely) level.

The top team spent considerable time discussing the issue, including whether the desire never to harm anyone during the course of their working lives was actually achievable. In fact, a big issue became whether people actually believed in the vision of "zero harm." This process of top team alignment took a while and some people left as a result of their inability to align with the vision. This was important as the process of generating Clarity at the top had revealed that not everyone in that team was committed to the goal. Thus, they were unlikely to act appropriately and, as a result, Clarity about the vision would dim. The CEO was quite clear that there was no room for non-believers and the board backed this all the way.

Having done that, it was important to gather data and to really understand the issues.

This required extensive stakeholder dialogue with trade unions and employees:

- Did they believe that it was possible?
- What were the issues/roadblocks?
- Did the contractors to the company believe it was possible?
- Were they prepared to commit?

This process took a lot of time and effort on the part of the top team and to demonstrate their commitment they did a lot of this dialogue personally. It wasn't neat, tidy or easy but it provided a much richer understanding of the issues and helped develop the roadmap. The process also engaged with a large number of people across and around the organization and, in the course of that debate, there was an increasing sense of commitment to the goal. It was also a process of building trust as, in the past, the unions and the management had used safety breaches as a weapon against each other.

The CEO was very committed to the vision and he identified one of his most experienced reports to champion the process. Fortunately, the person responsible was used to managing large complex projects and so he developed a very effective project plan to cover the building commitment phase. The main thrust of this was to get many hundreds of managers globally to not only believe but to develop the skills to manage complex change; in a sense this used safety as an opportunity to raise overall leadership capability and provided additional benefits.

Notably, the director concerned led very much from the front. He attended all the launch sessions, he was closely involved in the design, and his presence was an ongoing reminder that this was extremely important to the guys at the top.

To ensure that the Capability existed within the organization a significant budget was established and a toolkit of best practice and a training program was developed. Interestingly, while the toolkit was provided to the divisional managers they were expected to adapt it to their own needs and their own business cultures. But what was always clear was that they were absolutely accountable for delivering the results. So, the "what" was very much defined but the "how" was left to them within some clear parameters. This was a very effective approach in a very complex change challenge and the resultant distributed decision making rendered a huge multiplier effect within the firm.

Lastly, the company put great store by driving Consistency throughout the process. They made it clear they believed that a well-run, profitable business and a safe business were synonymous. So, you wouldn't be regarded as a successful manager if you had lousy safety results, and what is more you wouldn't get promoted either. Indeed the CEO went on record via a webcast saying that a manager with a poor safety record would not get promoted however good their other metrics were. This approach integrated what may have otherwise been seen as an initiative into the heart of the business. In so doing, it made being Constant in one's resolve, purpose and direction that much easier to achieve.

Case 2: Growing the Top Line

A division of a large regional business needed to rejuvenate itself. It had been focused hugely on reducing costs over many years but had ignored the revenue line; while profits had grown, sales revenue had been static.

A new CEO was brought in with the express purpose to grow the top line. Her first move was to exit a business that provided about half the revenues. Perhaps counterintuitively, she had spotted that its technology was outdated, and the competition was of much bigger scale and higher capability. Within the market, there was an opportunity to sell the business for a good price before terminal decline set in and eroded its existing market-worth. This was a big shock and in a sense it was the wake-up call that everyone needed. Post-sale there was a smaller, more profitable, and more focused business that was a clear market leader with a well-defined competitive advantage.

However, not everyone was so enthusiastic and so a process of changing out the top team commenced. In this case it wasn't a bloodbath but rather a careful and planned process to create a team of believers with higher capability than their predecessors. Over a couple of years nine out of ten people changed roles.

But the top team process was only a small part of a wider cultural change. The CEO and her team worked hard to create a compelling vision that was supported by six statements that defined exactly what the vision meant. The level of Clarity was high because the definitions were very specific but this CEO knew that wasn't enough. So her HR Director established a process that ensured that everyone's objectives cascaded down from the vision, which was accomplished through workshops that created sharp focus for all the white-collar employees.

Alongside this, the CEO made sure that every piece of communication made to employees was written or said in a manner that reinforced the vision and its six definitions. In a sense this was a propaganda process: every letter, newsletter, speech, presentation would be written through the lens of the vision. The CEO visited every facility every quarter and in a town hall meeting would talk about the company's performance but always in the context of the vision. And what is more, this was a process that went on for the whole of the five years that the CEO was there. Many years later, it continues.

Product development, sales and marketing were also defined through the vision. For the first time R&D and Marketing were working together to achieve a common goal. In some areas where the problem of change seemed more intractable, consultants were used to kick-start the change process but they were helping a process not supplanting it with their own.

After a couple of years, people on the shop floor also began to believe and had defined the vision in their own words and in a way that made sense to them. When measured in employee opinion surveys, they were as committed to the vision as the top team, which is the ultimate definition of success!

None of this was a quick fix; it took a couple of years to really engrain it throughout the organization even though it only had a few thousand employees across a couple of countries.

Summary

This gap stuff isn't hugely complicated but it does require close attention. Setting a strategy and developing a vision isn't difficult but does undoubtedly require a diligent approach. Asphyxiating the organization once a year with some hugely bureaucratic process is unnecessary and, having been done so in far too many organizations, is one of the main reasons that strategy has become slightly besmirched as a business practice. However, conducted in an effective, valid and practical manner, i.e. strongly laced with commercial realism and pragmatism, it can contribute significant value whatever sector it operates in. Strategy is not solely the province of private enterprise.

A senior leadership team that really understands the gaps between an accurate and honest current state assessment and where it wishes to be in five years' time begins to acquire competitive advantage for their enterprise. One that creates a well thought out idea of the roadmap to complete the transitional journey (one that is not rigid but has sufficient elasticity to absorb the bumps and shocks that will be encountered along the way – the only certainty is that there will be surprises!) gains further advantage. And one that also manages the whole process with rigorous and vigorous attention will gain still more advantage.

The process is the umbrella to the majority of change an organization will undertake because the analysis identifies the capital, structural, and human investments required. Successful physical capital investment projects are managed well, so must this process and those other critical change activities concerning structure and people. Working through the change by applying the principles of the Five Cs of Climate, i.e. Clarity, Commitment, Consistency, Constancy and Capability, improves the odds of success for the organization's leadership.

CHAPTER 6
Capability

Fundamental to any change intervention succeeding is the capacity of the change leader to lead the process effectively. Major change does not take place in isolation from the normal day-to-day activity of the enterprise. The whole of the organization's stakeholder population still needs to be engaged, whether that is customers served, staff managed and developed or suppliers used. The requirement of all senior leaders to "keep their eye on the ball" and to keep complex change programs progressing in such a way that they don't jeopardize "business as usual" is highly demanding. Particular qualities are required and it is these that we explore in this chapter. Our principal focus will be those change leaders at the top of the organization. However, the fundamental points that we make will relate to all levels.

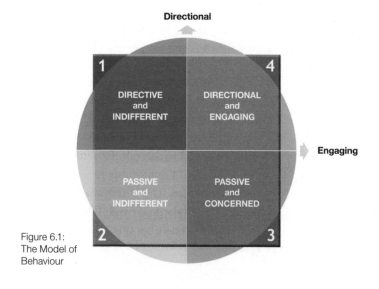

Figure 6.1:
The Model of
Behaviour

Returning to the Integrated Framework described earlier, we see at its fulcrum the leaders' behaviours and in Chapter 1 we positioned this concept of behaviour in terms of Blue 4 (see Figure 6.1). Senior leaders set the tone for everyone else in the organization and it is they who fundamentally create and establish the Climate. As the framework shows, behaviours contribute significantly to the quality of Organizational Climate. As we described in the previous chapters, Climate is the most significant differentiating factor between outstanding and average performance in the context of change. It is these conditions of Climate that are required in order to enable sustainable behavioural and attitude change.

Above all, if major change is to be delivered successfully, it is crucial that the organization's top team is of the right caliber. We have spent many years working with senior teams of different shapes and sizes from across all sectors and cultures and we know what is needed. Many times, after a couple of years into their tenure when things are not developing as they would like, we have heard CEOs express regret that they hadn't spent sufficient time during their first few weeks reviewing the capability of their immediate team. Their acceptance of "the okay", their desire not to upset the equilibrium, their need to be liked, or simply their failure to set high enough standards of performance has come back to haunt them. While CEOs need to have a vision for where they wish to take their organization, they must also be able to determine in their minds the manner in which their organization needs to be structured and how the roles in that structure should be populated. In other words, strategy, structure, people. Conversely, from research among FTSE 500 chairmen and CEOs conducted by Glowinkowski International Ltd, those CEOs who were enjoying success said the paramount reason was that they got their team organized and populated with real talent very soon after their appointment.

In this study, each individual commented that whenever they had initial doubts about an individual's capability or fit in the team, then nine times out of ten they were proved right. A frequent comment was, "I didn't think they would step up to the mark, and I was right. I should have let them go at the beginning."

Equally, we see the same consequences occur when CEOs recruit people in whom they had some doubt. Sacrificing standards, i.e. appointing someone who doesn't demonstrate the clear ability to hold down the defined role is a common problem either because the recruiters were in a hurry, or they didn't scrutinize their candidates hard enough or because the CEO doesn't wish to recruit people at least as able as themselves. This is not restricted to the private commercial sector. In an interview published by the *Financial Times* in June 2010, Barbara Stocking, CEO of Oxfam, the global charity organization, commented in response to the question "What has been your biggest work mistake?" the following, "Not getting rid of people soon enough. I give people too many chances." (Jacobs 2010)

For newly appointed managers whether at the level of team leader or chief executive, the recruitment and development of their team is without doubt their highest priority.

Team dynamics are complex but one certainty is that an effective team neither comprises a number of similar roles nor are those roles carried out by the same type of person. The best teams, whether in sport, communities or business, contain people of differing views, qualities and contributions and it is the blend of these diverse attributes that differentiates the great team from one that is simply average. A high-performing team needs to contain the right number of precisely defined roles that are occupied by individuals who possess the necessary range of capabilities to perform their responsibilities. Each role or individual by itself will not permit the organization to make its vision reality. Through effective leadership, the CEO aligns the accountabilities of every role to contribute explicitly to attaining the strategic goal and, crucially, enabling the role holders to understand that aim and how they personally contribute. This is Clarity and it is developed by the leader building Commitment through Consistent and Constant behaviour and communication. It is also an illustration of the CEO delivering Blue 4 behaviour.

Helping everyone across the organization and, in particular, the senior leadership team understand what they are there to do is not simply a case of "telling." The fact that the individuals are all different means they approach tasks, consider issues and engage with people in different ways and for different reasons. The CEO needs to help people understand these dynamics by using an approach that is both rigorous and practical.

What is needed is a means to help a group of individuals understand how they can harness their diversity and yet operate, behave and function in a mutually supportive and reinforcing manner to help steer their organization toward its stated aims. Where such harmony of approach between the senior leadership is not apparent, it is easy for those lower down the hierarchy to become confused and resistant to change. We are not saying there should be no disagreement within the senior team. Robust and vigorous argument is a mainstay of making well-considered decisions. An executive team that simply acquiesces to the CEO is not going to be truly effective, but ultimately there can only be one boss and once the decision is taken, collective accountability must prevail.

Diversity is an absolute asset to an organization but the causal factors and their consequences need to be appreciated. When they are, a team knows itself better. It knows its strengths and it knows where it may have deficiencies that can be closed either by development or by recruiting the requisite talent into the team. So often, we find organizations possessing an abundance of evidence on which to make financial decisions, sometimes too much. Conversely, we find organizations making decisions about their human capital almost entirely in the dark. These decisions can quickly undermine the apparent logic-based financial decisions.

In the next chapter we will focus on the issue of effective team working and the implications of successful change delivery. Here we concentrate on the issue of capability in a more generic sense. Our work in this area focuses upon using valid and practical measurement to provide a CEO and their immediate team with reliable, credible and actionable data about themselves and others across the organization. This "audit" will provide senior leaders with the means of avoiding giving the same answer as did Barbara Stockwell (2010) to the question about her biggest mistake.

What makes for a superior performing senior manager and change leader?

Over numerous years we have examined the question of what differentiates average from outstanding performance. This work has been conducted across cultures, work sectors and organization levels. In particular, we have studied the differentiators at senior and CEO level positions.

Take 100 CEOs who have a track record of success, where success is measured in terms of outcomes such as profitability, safety, production, brand reputation and, of course, the successful implementation of complex structural change. Compare them to 100 CEOs who have run measurably less successful organizations. Compare these two groups of individuals and the crucial characteristic that differentiates them is behavioural rather than factors such as skills, e.g. commercial business acumen, balance sheet management, knowledge, has run several M&As etc. These factors represent threshold rather than distinguishing characteristics, i.e. they are critical to have but they don't make someone outstanding. Consider the analogy of a highly qualified doctor: their academic credentials do not necessarily make them a great doctor but they need the academics to be a doctor.

Not only do we recognize the difference between superior and acceptable performance to be due to behaviours but we have identified a number of specific, discrete behaviours that really do differentiate performance.

From our analysis, some examples of the differential behaviours are listed in Table 6.1 below.

Table 6.1 Examples of Behavioural Characteristics which differentiate outstanding performing CEOs from average performers

The key differential is the ability of high-performing CEOs to think conceptually and over lengthy periods of time, which we respectively call Conceptual and Forward Thinking. For instance, being able to look at the broadest of themes at play in the geopolitical/economic environment and to break down this complexity into those issues that will affect their organization or, in certain instances, how their organization can affect those dynamics. Recognizing which natural resources are going to be wanted over the next quarter-century is vital to global enterprises operating in this market. Another is being able to consider a range of scenarios, e.g. political stability in source countries of those minerals, and preparing contingencies for such eventualities. In the straightened times of 2008-2013 another "thinking" behaviour has become a differentiator whereas previously it was threshold. This is Analytical Thinking, where the ability to rationalize and review the outcome of tactical decisions made upon broader strategy is key to managing the oxygen of survival, i.e. cash flow. In this sense, we see the highly effective CEOs demonstrating what we describe as "T-shaped" thinking, i.e. thinking both broadly and deeply.

Given that top talent is really tough and expensive to attract, we see the behaviour Developing Others being regarded as a differentiator. The CEOs who genuinely cultivate talent will equip their organization with the ability to withstand the tumult of the current economic turmoil as well as instilling appropriately risk-balanced opportunism. The organization will possess a well-structured succession plan.

Another distinguishing behaviour is Critical Information Seeking. This enables CEOs to establish information systems that provide insight into the forward-looking "vital signs" of the organization so that deteriorating trends can be quickly identified and corrected. Critical Information Seeking helps CEOs quickly and efficiently differentiate the urgent from the mass of data that assails them on a daily basis. In a natural sense, the very best CEOs we have engaged with have retained a child-like inquisitiveness. They frequently ask, "Why?" or **"How so?"**

The final four behaviours all reflect aspects of the way in which the CEO manages themselves. They speak out and are prepared to raise difficult issues with others (Independence); they persist and prevail in the most challenging of circumstance (Tenacity); they are open-minded and will listen and take on board others' views (Flexibility). They are also very focused on their own development; they recognize the need to continue to learn and to learn widely (Self-development).

The outstanding performers "think" and "do" more of these behaviours than the average performers. These behaviours or competencies are shown to be associated with outstanding performance. The key point is that we have demonstrated empirically that CEOs who deliver outstanding outcomes deliver statistically significantly more of these behaviours than average CEOs. A further connection to make is that these behaviours as a totality underpin the delivery of Blue 4 behaviour as described earlier. In this sense we can describe these behaviours as genuinely distinguishing characteristics.

Summarizing these past few paragraphs, we can represent the capability requirements that need to be considered in the form of a simple four-box model as shown in Figure 6.2. The change leader must ensure their senior team has sufficient capability across all four domains and, particularly, that the team possesses the full complement of behaviours to deliver successfully the required changes that are needed for the organization to achieve stated goals. Where there is imbalance or absence of the required behaviours, success is the less likely outcome.

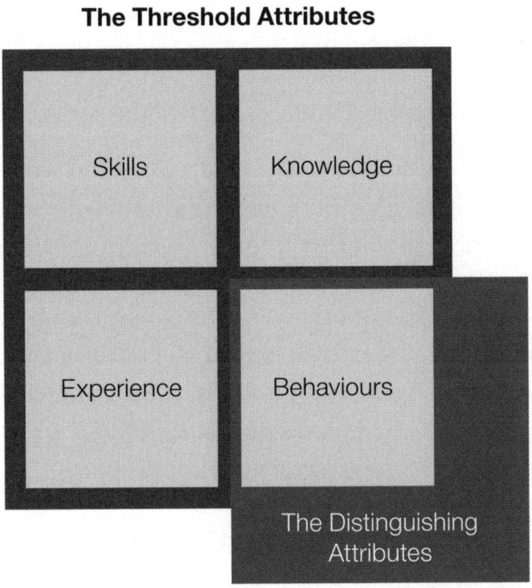

The Threshold Attributes

| Skills | Knowledge |
| Experience | Behaviours |

The Distinguishing Attributes

Figure 6.2 A Four Box Model of Capabilities

There are five critical questions to address:

1. Given the strategic aims, what formation or structure does the senior team need to possess?

It is interesting to consider here how a top-flight football team will go into different matches having different formations and those formations being populated by different players. It is the same in large organizations: what is the intent, what needs to be done, who can do it? In other words, what are the accountabilities of each role?

2. To deliver the accountabilities of each role in the structure, which specific skills, knowledge, experience and behaviours are required?

3. How long are the roles required for?

   Roles should not be considered to exist for perpetuity. When its accountabilities have been discharged it no longer needs to exist in the structure. And although the person who held that role has successfully fulfilled its accountabilities it does not mean he or she can simply be repositioned in the organization. The earlier sequencing of questions needs to be asked, i.e. what is the role, what does the person bring, is there a match?

4. What about the overall composition of the team?

   Do the team understand each other's roles and what each individual brings? Are there gaps of a particular attribute or an over-richness of one and how might this "blend" be complementary or jarring?

   In those instances, where we have worked with CEOs and their senior teams to explore these issues, the result is a far more engaged, collaborative and collegiate body of senior managers. Where such scrutiny is not conducted, we find the team can fracture quickly and, as a result, Clarity, Commitment, Consistency and Constancy are in short supply.

5. What is the ongoing potential of the different individuals?

   Not everyone around the top table can become a CEO, and most members of the team realize this fact. However, it is important that all members of the team understand how they are viewed, what is expected of them and whether or not they are likely to get the top job. Great CEOs try to develop their successor from within and this requires skill, sensitivity and a preparedness to have at least one person around the top table who, in time, could do their job.

We mentioned earlier our work investigating the key differentiating factors in terms of outstanding and average performance at the most senior levels. We represent this schematically in Figure 6.3 and it is predicated upon our assessment work over 35 years with many thousands of managers in the widest variety of organizational circumstances. Our four attributes explained earlier are applied in three areas of executive capability.

- First and foremost we consider **Behaviours**, in other words how do executives actually operate?

    o How do they think?

    o How do they engage with and influence others?

    o What do they do?

    o How do they manage themselves?

- How do they use their **Skills, Knowledge and Experience** to drive crucial management processes?

- At what **Level** have they operated? Here we are considering the intellectual complexity they deal with, and the length of time over which their decisions have impact.

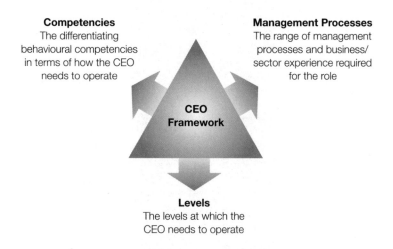

Competencies
The differentiating behavioural competencies in terms of how the CEO needs to operate

Management Processes
The range of management processes and business/ sector experience required for the role

CEO Framework

Levels
The levels at which the CEO needs to operate

Figure 6.3 Three sets of criteria for senior level assessment

The first element of the framework is a comprehensive behavioural model, which includes not just the behaviours listed in Table 6.1 but ten others as well. These 18 behaviours are grouped as suggested above into four clusters concerning Thinking, Influencing, Achieving and Self-management. As can be seen in Figure 6.4, these behavioural clusters are very clearly congruent with four main themes of leadership activity, namely:

- Developing Vision and Purpose (Thinking)
- Gaining Commitment (Influencing)
- Achieving Business Outcomes (Achieving)
- Managing Self (Self-management)

LEADERSHIP DOMAIN	COMPETENCY CLUSTER	INDIVIDUAL COMPETENCIES
Develops Vision and Purpose	THINKING	• Strategic Thinking • Conceptual Thinking • Analytical Thinking • Forward Thinking • Customer Understanding
Gains Organizational Commitment	INFLUENCING	• Strategic Influencing • Relationship Building • Inter-personal Awareness • Concern for Impact • Developing Others
Achieves Business Outcomes	ACHIEVING	• Results Focus • Concern for Excellence • Initiative • Critical Information Seeking
Managing Self	SELF-MANAGEMENT	• Independence • Tenacity • Flexibility • Self-development

Figure 6.4 – CEO Behavioural Framework

These behaviours or competencies have emerged as significant predictors of leadership capability through the many years of research that we have conducted. Put simply, the more effective an individual is in terms of their ability to Think, Influence, Achieve and Self-manage, the more successful they will be in their leadership contribution. We have found that outstanding performers with further potential exhibit strong capability within each of the competency categories.

It is this framework that underpins the 4 of Blue 4 in that the four categories of Thinking, Influencing, Achieving and Self-management (and the 18 component behaviours) enable the outstanding leader (and team member) to deliver directional and engaging behaviour, i.e. delivering Blue 4 rather than Red, Amber or Green. In forming their new team, it is critical that the CEO collects a robust appraisal of each candidate, be they in an executive role at the top table already or one level down the hierarchy or in their own external network. This assessment must be geared unemotionally to determining who provides the best fit to each role and how these individuals will gel and create a truly collaborative team.

The Management Processes

Ensuring that individuals measure up in terms of the 18 behaviours described above is, of course, critical. It is the possession of these behavioural qualities that truly distinguishes outstanding performance. However, on their own these behaviours are insufficient and need to be underpinned by the threshold characteristics of skills, knowledge and experience, i.e. those factors which are required for minimum performance and legitimize people being invited to the top table in the first place but don't necessarily mean they will be great leaders. We consider their application across nine crucial management processes that are shown in Figure 6.5 and explained in the succeeding paragraphs. Across the team, not everyone can be good at all of these but, collectively, the team needs to be able to demonstrate adeptness and skill at managing these activities.

Figure 6.5: The Management Processes

Business / Sector Experience

As we discussed with the Five Cs earlier, Capability is very important. The first and most obvious consideration is the importance of specific business sector and/or functional experience. This isn't to say that all of the team must come from within the industry; that is unlikely to satisfy the diversity point, but the basic skills and experience do need to be present.

The best teams tend to have a blend of seasoned professionals from within the industry, some "outsiders" to bring fresh perspectives and some functional experts whose experience is often a blend of inside and outside the industry.

Operational Change

This concerns the extent to which an executive understands how their enterprise's product, processes or services get to market. It necessitates understanding of the entire value chain from sourcing of materials to ongoing service support and maintenance.

Operational depth within the executive team will prepare it to deal effectively with a plethora of complex issues that arise. Change can be better planned, designed and implemented. It can imbue confidence down and across the organization that those at the top do know what they are doing. This can build Commitment.

Balance Sheet and P&L Responsibilities

Experience in managing an organization's balance sheet and P&L is a vital requirement for all executive teams. This does not just mean being able to compute the numbers; it means understanding their derivation and underlying meaning particularly in terms of quantifying the less substantive assets and liabilities a business may possess, e.g. brand goodwill, warranty exposure, exchange and interest rate hedges, disaster liability etc.

Included in the scope of this process are many regulations and compliance requirements, which failure to respect can have very significant consequences.

Such experience augments how executives apply their Analytical and Conceptual Thinking to manage their organization's financial dynamics. Crucially, this capability must not reside solely with the CFO; that in itself incurs a financial and operational risk. However, increasingly we encounter many senior executives who have not sought the opportunity during their career to acquire such skills and gain this very relevant experience (this is often due to the executive showing weak Self-development behaviour). They fail to recognize how these skills are important and, therefore, do not objectively set out to acquire them. In such situations, the ambition to become an executive is compromised by not possessing these abilities.

Risk Management

Risk management is distinct from managing the financial responsibilities explained in the previous point, although the two are inextricably linked. Failure to manage an operational risk can cause severe financial damage, e.g. consider major disasters that subsequent investigations attribute to poor risk management.

Risk management concerns taking stock of what may happen and what can be done to mitigate these possibilities. In the late 1980s and early 1990s, scenario planning was all the rage. Both technically and behaviourally through the delivery of astute Forward Thinking, such contemplation must once again be exercised by an organization's senior team. We have found those executives who are good at risk management possess an intuitive sense to investigate those situations where things appear too good to be true. They know such is unlikely to be the case.

Mergers and Acquisitions

Organizations' growth strategy is often based on acquiring other businesses, be they upstream or downstream in their value chain or competitors. In this sense, M&As are often a very important constituent activity in a CEO's change agenda. Fouling up an M&A can crash that agenda on to the rocks. Getting it right, particularly in terms of the integration of the two previously disparate teams, is of paramount importance. All too often, we find that immense time and effort has been spent in due diligence financially but far too little in terms of assessing the human capital. In this sense, expert knowledge of managing M&As is something else not to stack solely in the in-tray of the CFO. This is an area where an exceptional HR Director can add immense value.

As part of an expansion strategy based upon coupling organic growth with a program of M&As, the organization requires individuals who scan the market for potential acquisition targets and know how to bring these subtly into play. Inherent within an M&A strategy is a disposal game plan and the broad scanning will also identify potential suitors to which nascent, embryo businesses or more firmly established functions can be sold.

External Stakeholder Management

Effective stakeholder management enables organizations to operate in highly volatile situations that may be driven by complex political, social, economic, technological or environmental dynamics. Stakeholders include institutional and individual investors, suppliers, alliance partners, employees, customers, and communities hosting operations. With significant advances in information technology, we live in a connected world where a written communication that previously took weeks to circumvent the globe is now delivered immediately.

The need for senior executives to be astute and agile in their communication with their different stakeholders has never been higher. In terms of managing change through to successful implementation, the need to gather and respond to the views of all affected is very high in terms of building clarity for why the change must occur. This also means that for those whose commitment cannot be acquired, there is a plan in place to deal with their reticence.

It is because this skill is such an increasingly prominent aspect of an executive's role that we consider the behaviour of Strategic Influencing to now be threshold rather than distinguishing. Without such behavioural proficiency, the odds for delivering successful change are much reduced.

Business Growth

Building on but distinct from M&As and stakeholder management, we find ourselves in a business environment which demands a faster and more accelerated focus on the growth curve demands. Executives need to be able to harness the innovative capabilities of their people in order to achieve growth. This may be through more measured processes of continuous improvement or the potential to initiate more ground-breaking innovation.

This requires dexterity in managing the twin-tracks of day-to-day business and change in a manner that avoids jeopardizing either and enables the new of today to become the standard of tomorrow.

These skills are hugely enabled by an executive's strength in Developing Others, which provides for giving individuals with potential the opportunity to run their own business units. After initial conception and gestation, the new business is floated off from the parent, repaying the investment made. The more commercially astute research universities we encounter are doing some spectacular work in this area.

International and Multicultural

Understanding the cultural differences that prevail in different countries and social groups has become much more necessary in recent years. Failure to manage them can have grave repercussions.

The differences emerge at all levels, be they concerning ethnicity, age, gender, sexual orientation, disability, and social customs. Large global enterprises with which we have worked use development strategies for their senior executives that usually entail one or more overseas postings in order to provide real-time exposure to the cultural and social differences.

Closure (Redundancy)

Closure of business units and functions is part of organizational change. It is in these instances that the experienced executive will demonstrate real regard for their company's values in the way they treat those affected by any closure. Failure to do so will not only increase the possibility of industrial action as explicit resistance to the change but may also reduce the commitment of those who will remain because of the Cognitive Dissonance caused by promoting values but not honoring them.

We are not saying that experience in any of these areas is going to make the difference between an outstanding and average performance. We believe it is behaviours that drive this differential. However, these nine processes represent application of the fundamental skills, knowledge and experience required to drive change successfully and, dependent upon an organization's business model, one or more of these skills may become distinctive. Across the senior leadership team, all of the skills will be needed to a varying degree.

To provide readers with a benchmarking perspective arising from all of the assessments we have conducted across the FTSE 500 and large, complex public sector enterprises, we find it rare for a senior executive operating in such institutions to possess a really profound and in-depth ability in more than four of these processes (excluding the business sector experience). The average career span simply does not enable or permit this type of career breadth to occur. Therefore, any team will need to have a complement of these skills, knowledge and experience bases brought in by different team members. In this sense, the diversity of the senior team itself is a vital ingredient of success.

Level of Work

When two organizations combine, we see one of the incumbent CEOs or MDs step up into the enlarged role. While this may sate their ambition and personal power motivation, precious little scientific or practical consideration has been given to whether the individual possesses what it takes to operate in that much enlarged role.

Much work has been conducted in this area of level or rather the idea of role complexity. Put simply, an organization that sits at 250 in the FTSE 500 is probably significantly less complex than one which sits at 100 and even more so than one in the top 20. Figure 6.7 shows some criteria which is likely to increase the level of complexity in any role.

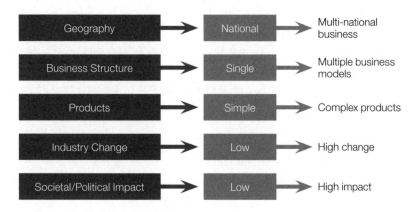

Figure 6.7 – Role complexity as affected by level

For example, an organization that engages internationally as opposed to nationally will have to contend with far more complexity. Even in domestic UK organizations operating across England, Scotland, Wales and Northern Ireland there are different national politics to navigate. Even if not operating in Europe, European regulations affect how organizations must function. In the U.S. there are numerous differences between states' laws and federal laws. Different countries bring different social values, mores and expectations. It is critical to evaluate the level of complexity that an individual has mastered in their career to date to assess the level of further potential that they may possess in the future.

Successful executives show three distinctive qualities. Firstly, they have the skills, knowledge and experience to manage the mission-critical processes for which they are accountable. Secondly, they possess the mental ability to deal with the increasing complexity, ambiguity and pace of a global economy. Thirdly and most importantly, they need to deliver the appropriate blend and profile of behaviours. **It is behaviours that provide the real and material difference between superior and average performance and fundamentally underpin their capacity to operate in a Blue 4 style.**

Recruiting the team

These criteria need to be measured and assessed in any recruitment process for a CEO or senior executive. Firstly, the role itself needs to be clearly defined in terms of its purpose and headline accountabilities. Then, in a practical manner, the candidates need to be taken through a process in which the three criteria can be considered. At its heart, this process should possess a structured, event-based behavioural interview that is conducted by trained interviewers. It is not an interrogation but it is a process that to be robust and valid needs to be conducted by trained professionals.

In many organizations, we find that above a certain level the processes used to select and appoint senior managers become rather flimsy. This seems especially the case in M&As where the acquiring organization, even in the instance of a smaller ascendant enterprise reversing into a more sluggish, established business, simply hefts out the existing team and installs its own. This "jobs for the boys" approach, while it may provide comfort to the CEO of the enlarged enterprise by allowing him or her to surround themselves with friends, usually presages failure of the deal.

It is vital to undertake an objective three-stage process, even though this may be painful personally or politically for the CEO. (This is where Independence behaviour is crucial; they can raise the sensitive issue with their previous colleagues.)

1. Design the organization and the roles in it based on a logical criteria of organizational need. Each senior role needs to be defined in terms of purpose and accountabilities and to set out the threshold and distinguishing (i.e. behavioural) capabilities that are needed. This will spell out clearly the processes for which the executive will be accountable as well as determining the intrinsic complexity and, thereby, level of the role.

2. To utilize a robust executive selection process that provides an accurate measure of two things.

a. Firstly, based on past behaviour and achievements, the extent to which the job applicant possesses the required capabilities in terms of competencies, processes and levels.

b. The extent to which the job applicant has the potential to develop the required behaviours, processes and levels in the future.

   We firmly believe that this can be achieved through rigorous, structured, event-based behavioural interview and assessment technique. In our experience, even when these processes are undertaken they are typically managed superficially; doing so will cause a catastrophic impact on any change program that necessitates the creation of new executive roles and selection of role holder.

3. Once the assessments have been completed and appointments made, the vital third stage is to engage in a comprehensive feedback process with each of the successful candidates (it is recommended to provide feedback to the non-successful candidates as well).

   No matter how talented the candidate is, some development need will always be identified. The feedback process enables the candidate to experience the motivational aspects of receiving positive, upside feedback concerning their strengths counterbalanced by them recognizing their gap areas, be they behavioural or skills-based. If subsequently the CEO then provides the executive with opportunity to apply their strengths concurrent with delivering a structured program of development to address their gaps, the pay-off in performance contribution is explicit, quantifiable and sustainable.

Here we have defined the characteristics required for outstanding change leaders in a generic sense. We know that in general terms each characteristic described can be shown to be associated with outstanding leadership performance. This can either be looked at in a distinguishing or threshold (skills, knowledge, experience) context – be it behaviours, processes or level. In terms of the Blue 4 model we know that the more the individual possesses and uses these qualities, the greater the chance will be of them demonstrating Blue 4 behaviour. This will create the Five Cs of Climate and therefore facilitate sustainable behaviour and attitude change with the change followers.

In this context the framework is legitimately aspirational, and while on one hand the chances of any single individual being outstanding across the piece is highly negligible, on the other hand it is important that individuals endeavor to play to their strengths as well as working to develop their abilities in the gap areas.

Of course we live in the real world and people will vary in their "capability sets."

John, for example, may be an excellent Conceptual and Analytical Thinker and perhaps highly experienced in the field of mergers and acquisitions. Janet on the other hand is highly Results Focused and driven by excellence. She couples these behaviours with her extensive experience in the processes of operational change and closure. Both of these individuals can bring tremendous strength to the team and in this example it may be that John's strength represents Janet's gaps and vice versa.

This is the reality of diversity within a team. Indeed, any CEO will require a blend of capability in a team and the management of this diversity in terms of creating successful team working is where we now turn. The next chapter considers capability from the perspective of outstanding leadership in terms of the collective team contribution.

CHAPTER 7

Developing the Team Behaviours

The importance of effective team working is self-evident and has been well documented over many years of practical application and academic research. The literature abounds with definitions of team effectiveness and numerous frameworks have sought to identify what the characteristics of outstanding team performance look like. The following are the most important when analyzing team effectiveness:

- Trust

- Openness

- Planned and systematic coordination

- Common purpose

- Collective goals

- Commitment to the values of the organization

- Balance and diversity of skills

- Awareness of each other

- Team members value each other

- The ability to raise difficult issues with each other

- Preparedness to address the difficult questions

- Constructive dialogue

In this chapter we consider the importance of team effectiveness with particular emphasis on the idea of a team delivering outstanding leadership as a team within the context of change. We are defining the executive team as the senior change leaders and that their effectiveness as a team will fundamentally drive the quality of their leadership both as a team (i.e. the collective leadership) and as individuals. The issues and principles that we present, however, will apply to all teams in the organization through any change program.

The focus of our approach is Blue 4 behaviour but in a team context. When a team behaves in a Blue 4 way it is collaborative and expresses to the broader organization a quality and consistency of leadership that drives the Five Cs of Climate in terms of Clarity, Commitment, Consistency, Constancy and Capability. Here we see excellent leadership behaviour and Climate within the team itself. This underpins the leadership perceived by the broader organization and therefore the performance Climate which generates the conditions necessary to achieve sustainable behavioural and attitude change in the change followers. This simple set of connections is illustrated in Figure 7.1

Figure 7.1: The connections between team behaviours and sustainable change

Shortly we will describe how the Blue 4 framework can be related to team behaviour, but firstly we want to consider some of the early work of Bruce Tuckman (1965) who back in the mid-1960s looked at stages of development in terms of small groups and teams. Tuckman came from an educational psychology background. He described four stages of group development. Through extensive research he examined the behaviour of teams and small groups in a wide range of different environments and situations. He identified four specific phases which they go through in order to achieve maximum effectiveness (Table 7.1).

Table 7.1 – Tuckman's four stages of Team Development

Tuckman's four distinct stages start as the team or group comes together and starts to operate. The process is essentially subconscious although he argued that an understanding of these stages can help group and team members achieve effectiveness far more quickly and less painfully.

FORMING. Individual behaviour is driven by a desire to be accepted by others and avoid controversy or conflict. Serious issues and feelings tend to be avoided and people focus on being busy with routines such as team organization, who does what, when to meet etc. The key objective of this stage is to establish things initially, to set things up and establish a basic set of routines and procedures. Individuals are also gathering information and impressions about each other, and about the scope of the task and how to approach it. This is often a comfortable stage to be in, but the avoidance of conflict and threat means that not much actually gets done and certainly difficult issues do not get addressed.

STORMING. Individuals in the group can only remain "easy" with each other for so long as important issues start to be addressed. Some people's patience will break early, and minor confrontations will arise that are quickly dealt with or glossed over. These may relate to the work of the group itself, or to roles and responsibilities within the group. Some will observe that it's good to be getting into the real issues, while others will wish to remain in the comfort and security of stage one. Depending on the culture of the organization and individuals, the conflict will be more or less suppressed but it will be there. We can see how the "easy street" of Forming can begin to turn into the "choppy waters" of Storming. To deal with the conflict, individuals may feel they are winning or losing battles, and will look for structural clarity and rules to prevent conflict persisting.

NORMING. As stage two evolves, the rules of engagement become established, and the scope of the group's task or responsibilities is clear and agreed. Having had their arguments, they now understand each other better and can appreciate each other's skills and experience. Individuals listen to each other, and are prepared to change preconceived views; they feel they are part of a collective, effective group. However, individuals have had to work hard to attain this stage and they resist any pressure to change, especially from the outside, for fear that the group will break up or revert to a storm.

PERFORMING. Not all groups reach this stage. It is characterized by a state of interdependence and flexibility, everyone knows each other well enough to be able to work together, and trusts each other enough to allow independent activity. Roles and responsibilities change according to need in an almost seamless way. Group identity, loyalty and morale are all high, and everyone is equally task and people orientated. This high degree of comfort means that all the energy of the group can be directed toward the task(s) in hand.

Tuckman would argue that effective teams break into Performing from the Norming stage if they address the issues they need to address. Poorer Performing teams may back off from addressing the issues and thus stay Norming (perhaps they fear reverting back to Storming) but in a way which is over affiliative and negative in style. Equally, poorly Performing teams may fall back into Storming as opposed to Norming and therefore become overly aggressive and coercive in their style.

Tuckman's original work provided an account of the way he observed teams or groups to evolve whether they were conscious of it or not. But for us the real value is in recognizing where a group is in the process, and helping it to move to the Performing stage (or indeed, keeping it at the Performing stage).

In the real world, teams and groups are often continuously changing. Each time that happens they can move to a different Tuckman stage. A group might be happily Norming or Performing, but a new member might force them back into Storming. Seasoned change leaders will be ready for this and will help the group to get back to Performing as quickly as possible. Many workgroups live in the comfort of Norming, and are fearful of moving back into Storming, or forward into Performing. This will govern their behaviour toward each other and especially their reaction to change.

Making a link with Blue 4 behaviour

We can make a link between Tuckman's (1965) original work and our own model of Blue 4 behaviour. This is shown in Figure 7.2. Storming is positioned in Red, Forming is positioned in Amber, Norming is positioned in Green and Performing is positioned in Blue 4.

A Team Building Process

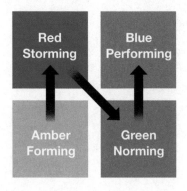

B Fast - Team Building Process

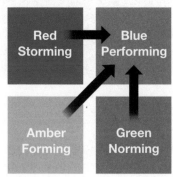

Figure 7.2 – A Route Map for Team Effectiveness

A key point in terms of the Tuckman framework is his developmental route map. He essentially argues that Amber is the start point, as the arrows show in Figure 7.2. We move through Red (Storming) through to Green (Norming) and finally into Blue 4 (Performing). This, however, is rather academic and from a practical point of view we can imagine all manner of routes to the goal of Blue 4. From our perspective we position Figure 7.2b as our key focus, so from wherever a group may originate the goal is to become Blue 4 (or at least more Blue 4). A little later we will build on this issue of development routes by considering the cultural issues that account for where a team may sit. Let us now consider team behaviour from a broad perspective of the Blue 4 framework.

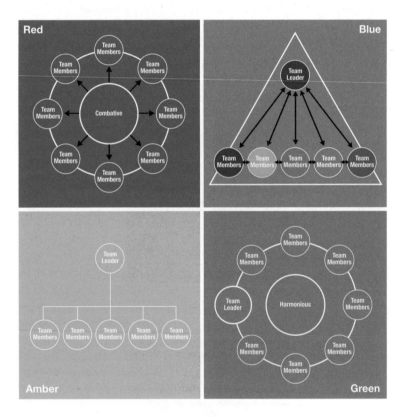

Figure 7.3: Illustration of the Team Behaviours

Figure 7.3 illustrates team behaviour from the perspective of Red, Amber, Green and Blue 4. Remember the two core dimensions are a combination of Directional and Engaging behaviour. Blue 4 represents behaviour which is

Directional and Engaging. You could argue that this also represents a balanced approach in terms of the needs of the tasks and the needs of the people. However it is positioned, Blue 4 represents functional and collaborative behaviour in the team with the remaining three colors representing various aspects of dysfunction. Our goal is to help teams understand their current behaviour with a view to developing and maintaining the extent to which they behave in a Blue 4 manner. The critical and practical objective is for teams to measure where they are and then take the steps and new learning in order to maximize their Blue 4 delivery. Let's consider the behavioural characteristics from each of these categories.

Red Teams

Red Team behaviour is described as a set of competitive and potentially aggressive behaviours. No one really doubts who the boss is and they are in the middle of everything that goes on. The style of leadership within the group is one of command and control where the link to the boss rather than between colleagues is emphasized. Competition and conflict within the group is the norm. The team's style of behaviour is assertive, dominant and noncooperative. It is characterized by argument and conflict rather than agreement and compromise.

Red behaviour generates a negative Climate within the team. The most significant outcome is a lack of Clarity with respect to the direction of the team, together with a lack of Commitment to the goals and objectives of the team which will almost certainly be dictated by the boss. Competition and conflict in a Red team is the norm. Sometimes Red teams perform well until the boss moves away and we see performance collapse.

Amber Teams

Amber Team behaviour is described as overly structured, bureaucratic and reflecting reticence in their behaviour to share views and be open with each other. The team tends to be formalistic in pattern emphasizing a quite impersonal approach. What is stressed are the lines of authority, the systems and procedures and its tendency is to be bureaucratic in its approach. There is a lack of communication and certainly a tendency of behaviour not to raise people's views and perspectives about key issues.

The team's style of behaviour is subdued with little or no communication among team members. Debate and discussion are stifled and not very forthcoming in capturing the real views of team colleagues. Members of Amber teams tend to keep their views to themselves and play their cards close to their chests. There is little focus in the team on the needs of team colleagues. The fundamental approach of an Amber team is adherence to the existing processes and procedures which determine who does what and how it is done.

As with Red, Amber has a significantly negative effect on the team Climate. Behaviour in the team is Passive and Indifferent and we will see this driving down each of the Five Cs of Climate. The negative impact on Clarity and Commitment is less to do with people being resistant to command and control (as in Red) and more to do with a general team leadership vacuum. In other words, their lack of opportunity for discussion causes Clarity not to develop and this lack of engagement will also undermine Commitment. This lack of engagement and communication within the team also poses a significant challenge to the development of Consistency and Constancy.

Green Teams

Green Team behaviour is described as overly affiliative and friendly and comprises behaviours that are about harmonious relationships at the expense of results. The circular pattern shown in Figure 3b.3 emphasizes the idea of harmony and equality of the team. The boss is essentially a team member and the process of running the team is based on goodwill. The most critical feature of a Green team is its rapport and this will be seen as far more important than the direction of the team, together with its systems and processes. Green teams are affiliative in their behaviour and while demonstrating care and concern for each other there will be little appetite to address difficult issues and provide uncomfortable feedback to each other. Green teams sweep issues under the rug and generate a tendency to avoid the difficult questions. The team's style of behaviour is to be predominantly friendly with each other. The key approach is one of affiliation toward team colleagues with a strong motive to avoid disagreement or hurting the feelings of others.

From a team Climate point of view we tend to see particular difficulties in the attainment of Consistency, Constancy and Capability. For example, we often see nepotism being practiced, friendship rather than performance being rewarded and where the focus is on the needs of the individual rather than the business. This will have a downward impact on the Climate dimensions of Consistency and Constancy. This lack of edge also impacts negatively the experience of Clarity (i.e. the "vacuum" syndrome). Eventually commitment to the organization disintegrates. We often find people describing a Green team as worse than a Red, because in Red "We at least know where we stand."

Blue 4 Teams

Blue 4 Team behaviour is described as truly effective teamwork which is inclusive of all team members and, therefore, engaging. The behaviour is collaborative, the team as a whole behaves with an appropriate balance of drive for results and concern for others. Figure 7.2b shows the true teamwork pattern which emphasizes structure, collaboration and inclusion. Blue 4 teams value openness and the team leader is ultimately the individual who takes and is seen to have the overall accountability but with the group behaving as a team and contributing their ideas fully. Blue 4 behaviour combines both task and people orientation. The style of behaviour in the team is characterized by openness and trust. Difficult issues will be raised, surfaced and dealt with in a constructive way. There is considerable debate as to the direction and focus of the team's short-, medium- and long-term direction.

It sets a Climate in the team which fosters an environment for people to reach their highest potential and works to strengthen bonds among team members. In our research we have shown that Blue 4 behaviour at the team level drives a performance-orientated team Climate. In other words, in the context of the senior change team itself, team members will feel a sense of powerful Clarity and Commitment to the organization together with a strong sense of Consistency and Constancy, in terms of what it feels like to be in the team. When this situation prevails, the scene is well set for individual respective team members in their own right as leaders to be more effective in their own delivery of Blue 4 behaviour and thus generate their own respective Climate systems.

How to create Blue 4 Teams

We have looked at Tuckman's (1965) work which provides an interesting developmental pattern for team behaviour and we have now linked that to our Blue 4 framework above. The key question relates to how a team is able to maximize its chances of performing in a Blue 4 manner whatever their current state may be. We have worked with many teams helping them to evaluate, measure and manage their team more effectively.

A set of profiles from three teams that we have recently worked with are shown in Figure 7.4. They are identified by their sectors. Using an assessment process of team behaviour we have indicated percentage splits for each of the teams in terms of the extent to which the four types of behaviour are delivered. From a practical point of view it is critical to understand the benchmarking thresholds for this type of behaviour. For instance, we know from our extensive database that a score of 75% in Blue 4 is at the threshold of outstanding team behaviour. Any score below 50% in Blue 4 represents a significant behavioural issue that prevails within the team. With this benchmark in mind we can begin to interpret the significance of these team profiles shown in the figure.

The profiles in Figure 7.4 are quite typical of the pattern of data that we observe in our work with teams. These indicate that all teams at any stage of their development will have a proportion of each "color" in their style. This is why an international benchmark is critical because it allows you to know, and therefore interpret, what is a real issue rather than just noise from a piece of behavioural data. Each of these profiles shows a Blue 4 score well below 75% which indicates that all of these teams have real work to do in order to raise their Blue 4 game.

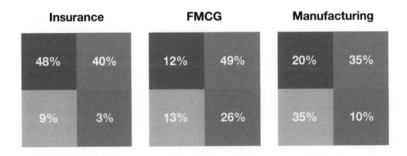

Figure 7.4. The Blue 4 Profiles for three teams

The insurance business scores 40% Blue. Their key issue, however, is too much Red behaviour. They are predominantly aggressive and competitive with each other and essentially overly command and control orientated in the way that they engage with the boss. Conversations that go on in team meetings tend to be between the boss and individuals rather than between individuals and the boss as a team. The flavor of the behaviour in team meetings is loud, competitive and combative in approach. There is little compromise and seemingly an approach where individuals strive to dominate the proceedings.

The FMCG Team scores 49% Blue which while significantly better than insurance is still way below the threshold requirement. Their key issue is too much Green behaviour. Their engagement as a team in characterized by an affiliative style and apparently strong set of harmonious relationships. There is little direction and focus for the team and difficult issues tend to get swept under the rug. During team meetings colleagues often indicate that they are supportive when in reality they are not. The team generally is low in its Clarity and only barely Committed to the apparently agreed objectives of the team. This team's key learning objective was to develop the ability to raise difficult issues and resolve them.

The manufacturing business scores 35% Blue. This is the lowest Blue 4 score in the three examples and represents quite a serious low level of collaboration and engagement as a team. The critical issue is the dominance of Amber which scores 35%. However, in addition the team scores significantly highly in its Red behaviour which is at 20%. At a general level team behaviour in this group is essentially indifferent and therefore they need to learn the behaviours of engaging each other in a more open and collaborative way. However, the 35% Amber certainly represents a situation where team members keep a lot of issues very close to their chest and this undoubtedly impacted Clarity within the organization.

We can see from these profiles that each of these teams had a need to enhance their Blue 4 scores but of course the particular development routes for the teams are different. Following the Blue 4 audit these teams began to consider how they might operate differently in terms of their core activities and behaviour. From a practical viewpoint these teams looked at their behaviours in terms of what we describe as the Team Clarities Framework. These Clarities or processes are as follows:

1. Strategy

2. Communication

3. Accountability

4. Relationships

Team Clarities Framework

We refer to this framework in terms of four team clarities which are illustrated in Figure 7.5 below.

The Clarities Framework captures the ideal of what effective team behaviour looks like in a practical context. This model is built on four critical team processes of Strategy, Communication, Accountability and Relationships. The Clarities isolate specific behavioural characteristics that are essential for a competent team to demonstrate consistently in the delivery of their business objectives for team success.

We have combined the Blue 4 Behaviour Model with the Clarities Framework in order to provide a tailored measurement of team behavioural style using the Team Performance Indicator. The indicator measures how teamwork is perceived and experienced by the team's own members in terms of the Clarities, and compares them with the perception of direct reports, colleagues and relevant others to create a holistic benchmark of teamwork behaviour.

The Clarities Framework	
Strategic	Strategic Priorities Establishing Direction Objective Setting Customer/Client Need
Communication	Within the Team With Stakeholders Managing Conflict Consistency of Communication
Accountability	Team Purpose Roles & Responsibilities Overlaps/Integration Support/Collaboration
Relationships	Team Relationship Stakeholder Network Achieving Mutual Benefit Team Feedback Review

Figure 7.5 The Team Clarities Framework

The Clarities and Blue-4: Strategic Clarity

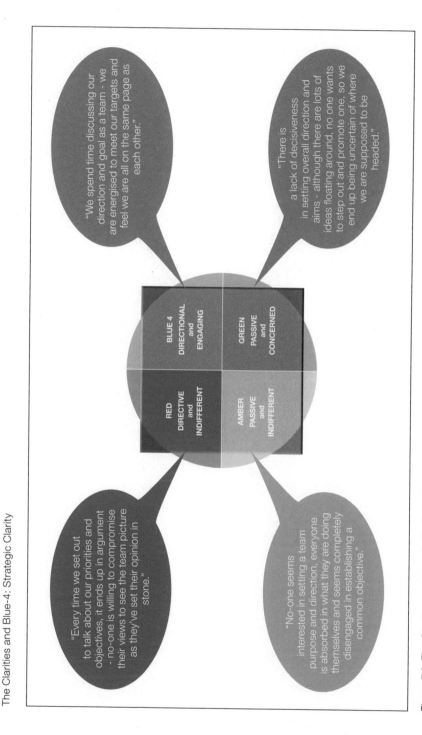

Figure 7.6: The Clarities and Blue-4: Strategic Clarity

The Clarities and Blue-4: Communication Clarity

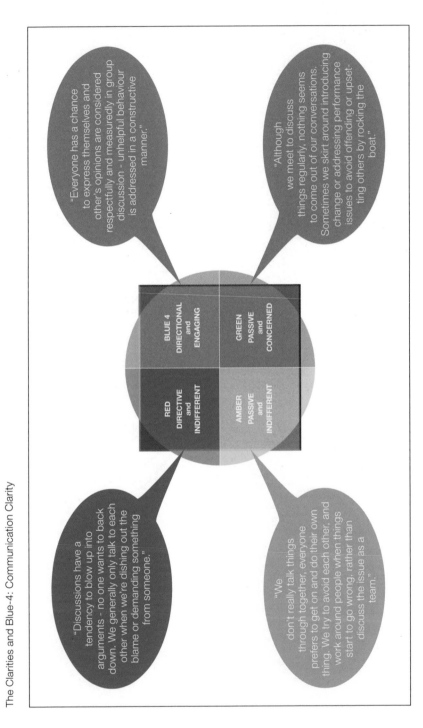

Figure 7.7: The Clarities and Blue-4: Communication Clarity

The Clarities and Blue-4: Accountability Clarity

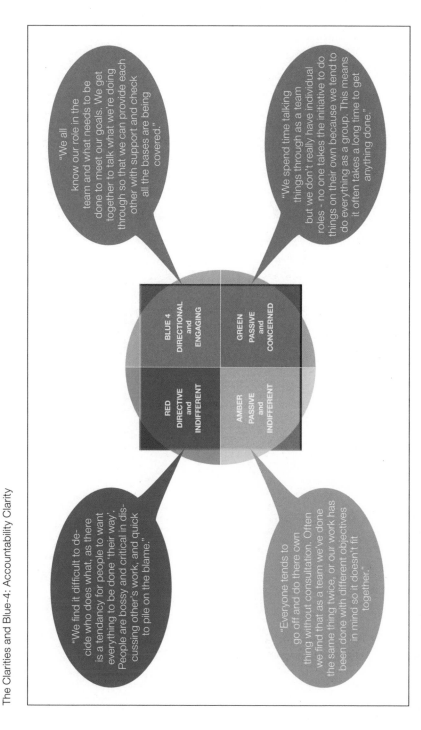

Figure 7.8: The Clarities and Blue-4: Accountability Clarity

The Clarities and Blue-4: Relationships Clarity

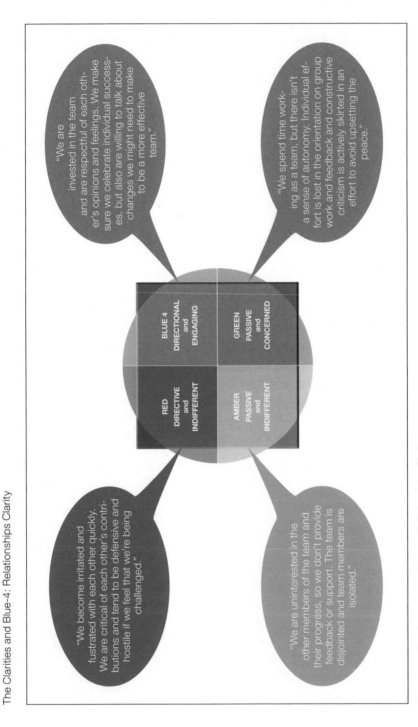

Figure 7.9: The Clarities and Blue-4: Relationships Clarity

136

What does good look like?

To provide a sense of benchmark, Figures 7.6 to 7.9 provide an illustration of exactly what Red, Amber, Green and Blue 4 behaviour actually looks like in the context of a team for each of these Clarities. From a qualitative perspective these frameworks provide an insight in terms of how it feels to work in a team whether it's predominately Red, Amber, Green or Blue 4. Adding to this, our database is able to provide a more quantitative analysis in terms of what actually constitutes a positive level of Blue 4. In general terms, we have found that Blue 4 behaviour underpins team performance which drives the business. The following points provide some further quantitative insights:

- Blue 4 behaviour needs to dominate each of the Clarities

- 75% Blue 4 is the threshold for team excellence

- Red, Amber and Green behaviour in the team is a business risk

- 15% or more for Red and Green is an issue for the team

- 10% or more for Amber is an issue for team

What Blue 4 scores actually mean

- 75% for Blue 4 reflects effective team performance with perhaps minor issues

- 50-74% Blue 4 reflects important team performance issues

- Below 50% Blue 4 reflects very significant team performance issues

- Below 25% Blue 4 reflects very major team performance issues and likely dysfunction

The actual performance connection

As we have seen, Blue 4 is associated with higher levels of business performance in a general sense. When we observe Red as dominant we tend to see an undermining of creativity, innovation and change. This pulls down performance in the business in many areas including product development, customer service and growth. When Amber is dominant we tend to observe an undermining of people's sense of direction, purpose and commitment.

This tends to pull down performance in areas such as productivity, sales, safety and long-term growth. Green behaviour is an overly passive orientation and this tends to undermine people's feelings of challenge, recognition and autonomy. It tends to pull down performance in areas such as retention of talent, standards of excellence and the delivery of results.

We were able to show that providing the teams with this type of data enabled them to have an open discussion about their behaviour in relation to the core activities and change to their mode of operation. With each of these groups we were able to demonstrate that the team was able to reshape their profile and enhance their Blue 4 score. Six months following the initial measure, each of the teams enhanced their Blue 4 into the 50% plus mark and this in turn drove a significant uplift in the Climate scores for each group.

The really interesting question is why were the teams like this? What were the key factors that caused insurance to have a predominantly Red issue, FMCG to be overly Green and manufacturing to be generally Indifferent but with a high Amber score? In fact, these type of results are not untypical with Blue 4 scores at or below 50% being more of the norm.

From our experience a whole raft of issues can underpin these types of profile results. Often it can be the culture of the organization or the leadership style of the boss. It may be the environment or circumstances in which the team finds itself. Often it is something to do with the nature of the team members themselves. In this context we have found that predispositions, which was discussed in Chapters 1 and 3, are highly significant. The predisposition profile of the team provides a powerful insight about why the team does what it does, what its potential strengths are, and what might be its major risks. Let's consider how predisposition influences and drives team behaviour.

Predispositions and Team Behaviour

In Chapters 1 and 3 we introduced the idea of predispositions or traits which help describe the concept of natural approach or "basic character" of the individual. While there are many different frameworks or models that are used to assess this area, we have adopted our own predisposition framework which is called the Global Predisposition Indicator (GPI™). The GPI™ was introduced in Chapter 3 and comprises the following five core dimensions:

1. Extroversion v Introversion

2. Collectivist v Individualist

3. Incremental v Radical

4. Flexible v Focused

5. Self-contained v Expressive

To use these dimensions in a team context we take the first four dimensions and create two pairs presenting them in the form of two 2x2 matrices. One of these is positioned as Problem Solving and Implementation Style and the other is positioned as Communication and Interpersonal Style and these are illustrated in Figure 7.10.

Problem Solving & Implementation Style

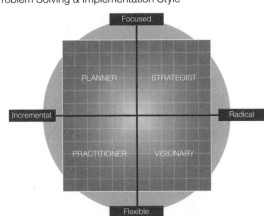

Communication & Interpersonal Style

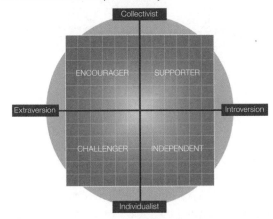

Figure 7.10. The GPI Problem Solving and Communication Frameworks

The Problem Solving and Implementation framework combines the Incremental/ Radical (horizontal) and Focused/Flexible (vertical) dimensions together as a 2x2 matrix. The matrix generates four quadrants. Moving clockwise these include the predisposition styles of Visionary, Strategist, Practitioner and Planner.

The Communication and Interpersonal Style framework combines Extroversion/ Introversion (horizontal) and Collectivist/Individualist (vertical) dimensions. The matrix generates four quadrants and moving clockwise these include the Supporter, Independent, Challenger and Encourager.

For application in team direction/building activities, the GPI™ is used to assess each team member's predisposition profile. These individual profiles can then be mapped on the 2x2 matrices thus providing a visual or picture of the overall team's predisposition.

Figure 7.11 shows a team profile for their Problem Solving and Implementation Style from the GPI™ framework. Here we see a team of seven people with five of them in the Visionary box and two extreme Planners. While all of these individuals may be of high intellectual capability the fact remains that from a predisposition point of view there are a number of potential significant issues that may block team performance.

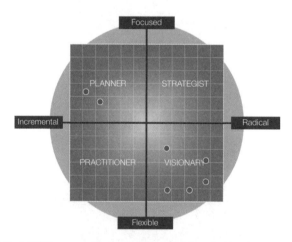

Figure 7.11: A GPI team profile for Problem Solving and Implementation style

In this example, the team's predominantly Visionary style lends itself well in terms of its capacity to generate new ideas but probably provides a weakness in terms of its capacity to deliver. Perhaps in forming the team, the CEO might have decided to create a more balanced group or, at the very least, if this was the team selected, the CEO must make the team aware of its collective style and the strengths and potential weaknesses this confers upon it. This awareness can help identify purposeful development each executive can undertake to improve the quality of engagement between the Visionaries and the Planners.

We often find that within such divergently styled groups conflict and difficulties do arise. The Visionaries regard the Planners as staid, boring and unwilling to change; the Planners tend to regard the Visionaries as unrealistic, disorganized and perhaps "off the wall." More realistically, we often see such a preponderance of Visionaries causing a real lack of Clarity in the organization because the flow of ideas results in what we describe as the "Grand old Duke of York syndrome": this week concerns going up the hill, next week everything is about going down the hill. In terms of getting the whole organization pointed in a unified direction, this is not going to be helpful. Any change program risks being subject to massive scope creep and veering off course.

From a behaviours perspective we often see a correlation between a Visionary-dominated team and Red behaviour. Visionaries are often impatient with their colleagues' lack of ability to recognize the value of their ideas. This is often exacerbated if the boss is one of the Visionaries. In this example the two Planners are likely to feel excluded – often their behaviour turns to Amber and they take their ball home and thus detach from the team.

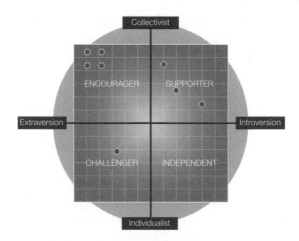

Figure 7.12 – A team GPI profile for communication and interpersonal style

Another GPI™ example profile is shown in Figure 7.12, namely the Communication and Interpersonal Style framework. The profile shows eight team members, three of whom are in the Supporter category and four in the Encourager group with one individual positioned as Challenger. In this example we again see a highly skewed profile. The vast majority of team members are Collectivist in nature and we often observe this style of behaviour underpinning an unwillingness to address issues, particularly of a personal nature. The style of the team is often highly Affiliative and perhaps overly people orientated. The upside might be an orientation to focus on people issues and to be highly engaging but the downside might be a lack of propensity to make the tough decisions. We sometimes see this type of profile underpinning a team's behavioural style that undermines the Climate dimensions of Consistency and Constancy. Life can also be difficult for the individual positioned in the Challenger box because they are likely to be seen by their colleagues as difficult and uncompromising. In turn, the Challenger sees their colleagues as somewhat weak and reluctant to grasp the nettle.

From a behaviours perspective this profile has some fascinating possibilities. At a general level the team is likely to be highly Green in its style with harmony and affiliation being the dominant drivers. It may have little edge in addressing issues openly and the potential for a relatively modest focus and direction. A key issue is where the boss sits. If they are "north" then the above behaviour is highly likely. However, if they happen to be the Challenger indicated in the profile then their behaviour has all of the potential to be strongly Red with the rest of the team behaving in a highly submissive mode – probably Amber. This situation is likely to be strongly exacerbated if the boss also happens to be a Visionary.

In looking at these team profiles, we haven't indicated which data point is that of the CEO, which in itself will have a considerable impact upon team dynamics. For instance, consider the CEO to be a Visionary/Challenger. It is likely he or she will be quite demonstrative in putting forward their ideas and, perhaps, a little reluctant to receive and accept feedback. Conversely, if the CEO is a Planner/Challenger, he or she may want to see a fine level of planning, checking and controlling conducted. As can be seen, many combinations are revealed by these team profiles. Well-facilitated discussion can help the team appreciate its underlying dynamics and start to surface in a safe environment the issues that have to be addressed if the team is to be successful in achieving its aims. Operating in the absence of this information leaves a team somewhat in the dark about its inherent strengths and weaknesses. It is unnecessarily handicapped in its competitive marketplace.

These types of profiles are in no way unusual. We see such skewed profiles regularly. In retail banking, we typically observe relatively Collectivist profiles, whereas in investment banking the profile is more Individualistic as it is in manufacturing and engineering. In the insurance sector, particularly when it's actuarial led, we see many CEOs being Planners in their Problem Solving and Implementation style coupled with being either Supporters or Independents in their Communication style, i.e. more introvert so energized by their own company rather than that of others.

The Change Dynamic: The Villagers and Nomads Case Study

We have collected predisposition data from a vast array of leadership teams involved in driving change programs. In most cases these teams are often formed with change in mind. They invariably consist of new appointees from outside the company and a number of longer time served individuals.

One recent piece of work that we were involved with included a senior management team from a UK-based food company. Figure 7.13 shows the predisposition data of this senior management group (including the managing director). Eleven of the team can be defined as long time servers (i.e. with the company for more than five years) and nine were new appointees that had been recruited with the change program in mind. The aggregated profiles differentiate each of these groupings with red dots indicating the longer time served group and blue dots indicating the new appointees.

Problem Solving & Implementation Style

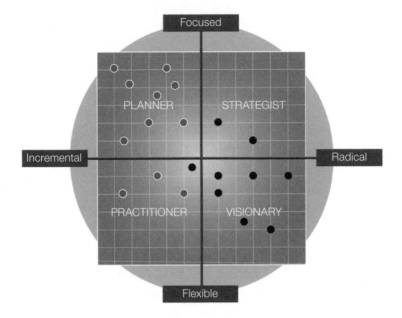

Communication & Interpersonal Style

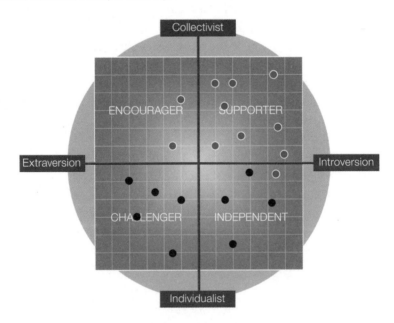

Figure 7.13: GPI Profiles for The Food Company senior management Group

The issue for this company was simply that their change program "just wasn't working." The newly recruited group spoke of "resistance to change" and "stuck in the past." The longer servers group spoke about their experience of being ignored and a feeling that the new appointees were generally aggressive and not really interested in their contribution.

What is interesting here is to consider the two profiles of these respective groups. In the context of Problem Solving and Implementation the new appointees are predominantly Visionary in style compared to the long servers as predominately Planner/Practitioner. In terms of Communication and Interpersonal Style the long servers are essentially more Collectivist with new appointees and mainly Individualist. In many respects the respective group's perception of each other is entirely predictable in the sense of natural differences being perceived in pejorative terms. The team's behaviour profile was only moderate in terms of Blue 4 with a dysfunctional picture of too much Red and Amber behaviour.

Perhaps what is more interesting, however, is the consideration that this set of profiles is not that unusual and often observed within similar management groups undertaking major change programs. We can perhaps assume the following key points:

- Long servers in a company, by virtue of their predisposition (i.e. more likely to be Planner/Practitioner) are highly likely to be more incremental in style – and less predisposed to move from one company to another.

- On the other hand, new appointees with a tendency to be more Visionary in style are much more likely to be predisposed to move more frequently from one company to another.

- Also, given that the Collectivist profile is associated with relationships and attachment, it is further assumed that the long servers profile also comes with that territory of "more likely to stay than move" with the converse being the case for newly appointed types.

- Most change programs are highly likely to have this dynamic almost built into their fabric.

In this context, we refer to these long servers as the "Villagers" and the new appointees as the "Nomads." In reality, these different sets of natural predispositions should be a positive, bringing different sets of skills and experience to the change program. However, in our experience and indeed as indicated in this Villagers and Nomads case study, the reverse often turns out to be the case. In the negative scenario we have the Villager group who feel generally undervalued by the new people coming in (i.e. the Nomads) where the Nomads themselves feel that their contributions are blocked and unwanted, causing frustration and impatience with the pace of change. The result tends to be a predictably Red and Amber behavioural state and this of course entirely undermines the change agenda.

Our basic assumption, and indeed practical experience, is that most change programs will be constituted with these types of differences, which in turn provide the basis for the type of dysfunctional reactions that we see in this case study.

This chapter has focused on the issue of the quality of teamworking within the senior change leadership team. We have concentrated on the idea of Blue 4 behaviour being representative of outstanding team behaviour where the behavioural style of the team becomes one of collaboration with the appropriate degree of focus on the needs of the task and the direction of the organization together with the needs of people and the concerns they may have. This style of behaviour within a team is both inclusive and engaging and highly likely to generate an outstanding level of performance Climate within the team. This in turn will underpin both collective team leadership and respective individual leadership toward the broader organization which will create the Five Cs of Climate within the organization as a whole.

We have worked with many teams using this framework and have demonstrated a team's capacity to reshape or remodel its behaviour in the direction of Blue 4, and this can be achieved at whatever stage of development the team may be at. A critical element in achieving this is to utilize the methodology of predisposition. This enables individuals and the team as a whole to develop a powerful understanding of who they are as individuals and the implications of that in the context of the overall team dynamic. We briefly consider above two relatively simple examples in terms of problem solving and communication and we can see how these patterns of predisposition can generate deviant or dysfunctional behaviour in terms of Red, Amber and Green. Helping a team to understand this dynamic enables it to move toward the direction of Blue 4.

CHAPTER 8

Development

The central tenet of this book is that the behaviour of the manager is a critical determinant of the Organizational Climate that ensues. The Climate of an organization undergoing profound change is defined in terms of the Five Cs, namely Clarity, Commitment, Consistency, Capability and Constancy. If these facets of Climate are strong, the extent to which the organization's broader workforce will feel motivated to delivering discretionary effort toward achieving the goals of the change program will be far more durable. Without asking, that awkward glitch discovered in the user-acceptance testing of the organization's new core IT architecture is resolved. People go the extra mile. If it were Disney, they'd say Walt had been sprinkling his pixie dust around the place.

There is no magic, of course, but rather it is the leaders' behaviours that are setting the behaviour of everyone else. The sullen leader (Amber) will create a sullen mood. The fair but firm, tough-love leader (Blue 4) will create a mood of determination, openness and purposefulness.

We are choosing our words carefully because we do not want to fall prey to grandiose yet meaningless terms. The fundamentals of leadership are more grounded and straightforward. Quite simply, what leaders do and how they do it has huge impact upon both the culture and Climate of the organization (Olson 2008). If this is healthy, people will go the extra mile; if it is poor, then at best they will just deliver the bare minimum with consequences for the quality of both employee and customer engagement. How things are done, i.e. culture, particularly change, is affected. Where Climate is strong, change is planned in an inclusive manner, managed effectively, implemented on schedule and within budget and the whole process is reviewed afterwards for points of learning. Where Climate is weak, change is poorly planned and through scope creep and other mistakes it is delivered late and doesn't work. Budgets soar, and the impact on the customer is detrimental. Leadership determines whether change is delivered successfully or not.

So what do we mean by leadership? How will it actually work in creating effective employee engagement? In this chapter we look at how to drive the Climate through the process of leadership development.

The Behaviours that Drive Engagement

From our research, we have identified six broadly defined behaviours that a leader needs to deliver in order to build and sustain performance-focused engagement with everyone in their organization. In this sense, leadership is a 360° process which in itself is an incredibly important point. Leadership is NOT in itself a behaviour or competency. It is a managerial process, which is effectively discharged by delivering certain behaviours when engaging across the entire stakeholder body. For instance with their boss, e.g. the CEO to Chairman; their peers, e.g. fellow executive committee members; and their direct reports. It also extends beyond the boundary of the organization into external communities such as customers, suppliers, partners, and the social communities in which the business operates.

The six broad categories of behaviours are:

1. **Setting and communicating the organization's purpose and future direction**

   Concurrent with doing this is the need to establish congruent and aligned goals and objectives for their people. The achievement of these will contribute to the organization achieving its aims. This behaviour is crucial in building Clarity and winning Commitment.

2. **Addressing issues and resolving difficulties as they arise**

   Issues need to be tackled at the right time. Either allowing molehills to grow into mountains through prevarication or jumping on the merest hint of a problem are not desired behavioural qualities. People do need to know where they stand in a firm, fair, open, honest manner. Having built Clarity around what is expected, this behaviour supports Consistency and Constancy and provides a firm base for Capability.

This behaviour will facilitate the development of open, honest, mutually supportive relationships right around the 360° network a leader must nurture and maintain.

3. Doing their own jobs not those of their subordinates

This is not to say they abrogate responsibility for what is being done; in fact the complete opposite is required but not to the extent of them doing the actual work itself. The Chief Marketing Officer shouldn't be writing marketing copy!

In a well-structured organization, it is clear at which level of work every role is positioned. The headroom between a manager and their subordinates needs to be considered carefully so that there is sufficient distance to differentiate the roles' respective responsibilities. This enables effective and efficient delegation to occur. This type of positional behaviour is absolutely essential in building commitment because direct reports feel a genuine sense of challenge and that their manager isn't perched on their shoulder checking on everything they do. People feel trusted, which is so critical to building a healthy Climate and of course absolutely fundamental to the development of Capability.

4. Engaging with their stakeholders and influencing them

Managers tend to understand the necessity to accomplish their assigned tasks but do not necessarily appreciate that the majority of them require the contribution of effort from others to be completed. Possessing presence and credibility, which does not mean being gregariously charismatic, will make it far easier for the manager to engage with their colleagues and gain their support.

It is worth making the point that in an organization characterized by its strength of purpose, winning support from colleagues becomes an exercise in mutual reciprocity because everyone recognizes how what each other is doing is clearly aimed at attaining the organization's aims.

Furthermore, this behaviour compounds the benefit of the previous behaviour. Where managers are doing what they are paid to do and they engage effectively, a truly collegiate focus will prevail. Commitment will grow exponentially.

5. Involving others in decision making and sharing appropriate information

Leaders must involve others in decision making whenever and wherever this is practical. Clearly some decisions cannot be made "in committee." However, consider those leaders who try to introduce changes to how their organization serves its customers without consulting with those who serve them directly are likely to be on a hiding to nothing.

Also, leaders need to share information with their people that is applicable to what they do. Telling everybody everything in the spirit of openness and transparency can be counterproductive. This, together with an ability to share things appropriately with others, not keeping information overly close to their chest, is crucial.

There is a fine balance to be struck between appearing coercive and being motivational. The manager who gives instruction and expects immediate compliance has zero chance of retaining the commitment of their team members. The manager may feel they have averted a crisis but the aftermath from those they have ordered around can be resentment about being bullied. In these litigious times, an organization can quickly be submerged under a swathe of grievances and associated tribunals.

Managers must recognize that using an appropriate democratic and inclusive process with their employees is the best policy to maintain Clarity and Commitment. Democracy ebbing and flowing with autocracy, however, will do nothing for Consistency and Constancy.

6. Developing talent

Leaders need to let their people know how they are performing. They need to coach their people to build their short-term performance. They need to engage in open, honest discussions with them about their long-term potential and development needs.

The "manager as coach" leads through inspiring others to excel. Coaching is actively sought rather than being regarded as the first step on the disciplinary ladder – we say "Coaching is for experts!" Within this, however, honesty must prevail and if someone is not cut out to do the job well, they must be removed. If people have Clarity about what is expected from them, seeing others get away with doing things poorly or not at all will quickly dull that Clarity and thereby Commitment and undermine the employee's perception of the Climate dimension of Capability. While this is painful, the individual will be grateful in the long run. It is also an essential extension of what we were saying in Chapter 6 about forming the senior management team. A disciplined, structured approach will always pay far higher dividends than currying the favor of friends.

Theme of Behaviour	How the change leader needs to consider their behaviours and accountabilities to their immediate team
DIRECTIONAL Establishing and communicating the direction	A team to whom I need to provide clear, concise and consistent explanation of what is to be done and why but not necessarily how as this may patronise and limit the discretion the team may feel they possess.
CONSTRUCTIVE Managing conflict and surfacing/sorting the issues	A team with whom I must build open, mutually respectful relationships alongside those that I must develop upwards, laterally and externally to the organization. These relationships are characterised by an openness and honesty that permits issues to be surfaced and resolved without causing animosity and any lingering grudge that will risk jeopardising completion of the change agenda.
POSITIONAL Working at the right level with effective delegation	A team whose skills and expertise I must respect and utilise to the full, delegating duties and tasks wherever possible so enabling me to concentrate upon my leadership and managerial responsibilities and avoid getting drawn into the minutiae that the team is entirely capable of managing themselves.
ENGAGING Being influential and having impact	A team with whom I need to engage in an entirely non-disingenuous manner so as to build respectful presence and credibility. A similar style of engagement is required across all my other stakeholder groups, including my own boss, their boss, my peers and external groups including investors, suppliers and customers.
DEMOCRATIC Involving others and sharing information and being open	A team whose confidence I must inspire by sharing appropriate information at the right time, whose ideas, thoughts, observations and feedback I seek regularly and thereby do not tend to coerce to get things done by orders but by their being inspired by the challenge I have set and the clear trust I demonstrate in their ability to get things done.
DEVELOPMENTAL Coaching/Developing and raising others capability	A team comprising eager to learn individuals who wish to deepen their skills, knowledge, expertise and behavioural competencies. The team regards themselves non-arrogantly as an academy of future leaders, who while learning achieve exceptional results.

Table 8.1 summarises the preceding paragraphs

From our experience, leaders who deliver these behaviours deliver enhanced business performance as a result. They engage in a far more proficient (and, indeed, professional) manner with their colleagues and other stakeholders. This enhanced quality of engagement contributes markedly to their creating and maintaining a stronger, more results-orientated Climate. They achieve through others; they actually lead!

From having assessed many thousands of senior leaders, we know it is possible to assess their current and potential behavioural capability. Having provided feedback it is then entirely feasible to establish a learning development plan that will help them raise their game. This applies to *all* leaders at *all* levels. In other words, through such a development process, leadership capability can be enhanced to permit the desired culture change to occur and drive up business performance.

The rest of this chapter describes how a behavioural framework can be used to facilitate such a development process. Within this explanation, we later consider a number of real life case studies that show this linkage between enhanced leadership behaviour and bottom line performance in terms of a major change program.

Linking the Behaviours to Blue 4

We described a number of important leadership behaviours in the previous section. Here we take these themes and convert them into our Blue 4 framework that can be used to measure leadership behaviour and form a basis for its development and improvement. We have taken the six themes and positioned them in terms of the two overall dimensions which make up the Blue 4 framework.

The first dimension relates to the manager who provides direction, focus and drive to get things done together with a capacity to operate at the right level rather than becoming overly involved in the extraneous and irrelevant detail. This represents an aggregation of Directional, Constructive and Positional behaviours shown in Table 8.1. We describe this summary as directional leadership behaviour. It is Forward Thinking, Results Orientated, Focused and addresses the issues.

We aggregate the remaining behaviours listed in Table 8.1 of Engaging, Democratic and Developmental to represent a behavioural style that is highly people orientated. It takes on board the views of others with a preparedness to listen and understand people, together with a focus on their development and growth. We refer to this aggregate as the Engaging dimension of the Blue 4 framework.

The two dimensions of Directional and Engaging are shown again in Figure 8.1. Let's consider the framework from a Leadership of Others and Engagement perspective.

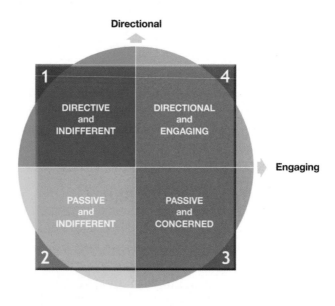

Figure 8.1: The Model of Behaviour

Red quadrant

This represents the combination of Directive and Indifferent behaviour. Here, while a manager sets out clearly what is to be done, they do so in a stern manner. Such managers are likely to be perceived by others as overly controlling, aggressive and abrasive, with a tendency to tell rather than listen. As a leader or, indeed, more generally as a team member, it is never effective to be Indifferent. The old adage of "being given two ears and one mouth and using them in that ratio" is entirely apposite.

Red therefore falls short of effective leadership and engagement behaviour.

Amber quadrant

This combines Indifferent with Passive behaviour. The probable perception by others is of a manager who avoids and abrogates, is disengaged, and possibly somewhat aloof. Generally, this behaviour will elicit a sense of the manager being a negative individual.

Amber is entirely dysfunctional and, therefore, never appropriate in a leadership and engagement context.

Green quadrant

This brings together the behaviours of Concerned and Passive. While being people orientated by virtue of the Concerned dimension, this style lacks the necessary drive or focus for action. Furthermore, issues tend to be left unaddressed and unresolved. Green is about pacifying and accommodating the needs of others. On one hand, the Green manager delivers a warm and engaging style, striving to be liked, but ultimately failing to make things happen. The same applies across team colleagues where harmony is sought at the expense of tackling important matters. Green behaviour can engender a lack of trust in others and cause rebellious repercussions because people don't know where they stand.

Like the previous two styles, Green is ineffective from a leadership and engagement perspective.

Blue 4 quadrant

This is the combination of the Directive and Concerned behavioural styles. From the former comes a focus on delivering objectives together with a capacity to address issues in a timely manner to establish openness and transparency. Also, the manager operates at the right level and delegates effectively.

The latter quality encompasses a genuine interest in others that focuses on their development coupled with a capacity to involve them in decision making and to value such contributions. Importantly, Concerned should not be regarded as conferring a soft, munificent approach. Rather, the developmental focus lends a harder edge in terms of being prepared to consider the ability of an individual to do their given job and to take action where there are shortcomings. The Concern arises out of recognizing that an individual who feels out of their depth will not be happy but may not be willing or able to admit this to themselves. Having a Concerned manager will see the matter identified, addressed and resolved. While there may be some initial pain, we have always found that such individuals so handled by their managers are grateful in the long run.

From a leadership perspective, a manager behaving in a Blue 4 style will be fully delivering all of the behaviours discussed at the beginning of this chapter and outlined in Table 8.1.

We are confident from our knowledge and experience of dealing with thousands of managers to contend that Blue 4 behaviour is entirely appropriate within any form of human interaction where problems need to be solved, issues addressed and a determined, collaborative atmosphere needs to prevail. Blue 4 behaviour is the name of the game if you want to create an effective leadership culture that will drive significant, strategic, structural change. Effectively delivering Blue 4 behaviour demonstrates genuine strength of Emotional Intelligence (Goleman 2000), which raises the quality of engagement individuals have across their stakeholder network.

The term "Blue 4 culture" embraces the outcome of consistently and constantly delivering Blue 4 behaviour. In other words, as we have said in previous chapters, the idea of Blue 4 culture represents how things are done (in this case the style of leadership), and this drives a Climate in which people *feel* (or experience) Clarity, Commitment, Consistency, Constancy and Capability.

In particular, the Directional aspect of Blue 4 generates Clarity in people's minds; they will have a far greater sense of what's expected of them and why. The Directional aspect also drives Consistency, simply because people will know what fits and what doesn't fit in terms of the game they're playing. The Engaging element of the Blue 4 framework will have a particularly powerful impact on raising Commitment as it is the behaviour which engages people's hearts and minds and, therefore, creates a better sense of buy-in about what the organization is trying to achieve. Similarly, Engaging behaviour generates Constancy in people's minds because the leader's effort to involve is not sporadic. Instead, their concern to avoid confusing their people, which will do little other than undermining their directional intent, means they engage with appropriate regularity. Too much constrains discretion, too little blurs Clarity. It is a fine balance but one that can be achieved through development and practice.

Model, *M*easure, i*M*plement

In a very practical sense we have established a viable three-part development process that when followed provides a very significant fillip to the likelihood that the change program sponsored by the CEO or other board or exco official will deliver on its promises. The sequential process we label *M*odel, *M*easure, i*M*plement or MMiM for short.

Model

Here, we refer to the Model of Behaviour shown throughout this book and referenced above together with the Integrated Framework shown earlier. The representation of the four different behavioural styles in the Model of Behaviours is based on extensive research with many thousands of managers from across sectors, levels and geographic locations. It is a framework that has the required statistical validity that possesses the necessary underpinning of any model that is to be taken credibly rather than with a pinch of salt.

The model provides a benchmark of excellence and the platform on which a common language can be used across the organization. There are no ambiguities to the term so it is more readily understood and, therefore, practiced. This lends the model practicality.

The model's clear and explicit fit with the behaviours considered within the Integrated Framework is substantiated by large amounts of data we possess that confirms the correlation between Blue 4 behaviour, strong employee engagement and a healthy, vibrant, performance-orientated Climate. As the starting point to any change initiative, Model is critical. Quite frankly and quite simply, people get it because the concept is valid and practical.

Measure

The second part of our approach is measurement: "If it can't be measured, it can't be managed (or changed)." It is so important to have the capacity to measure the extent of Blue 4 behaviour at either the individual or the organizational level because it enables people to know where they currently stand and how, as a result of development, they are improving. Blue 4 measurement is conducted through an online 360° survey, which provides an individual with a quantitative indication of the degree to which they deliver Blue 4 behaviour in four crucial managerial situations: Setting Direction and Objectives, Communicating, Decision Making, Performance Management. The 360° data profile provides an individual with their own view of their engagement style as well as that of colleagues, e.g. their boss, their peers and their subordinates. In this way, in a very real sense, "beauty is in the eye of the beholder."

An example of the feedback is presented in a pie chart format, as indicated in Figure 8.2.

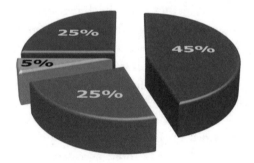

Figure 8.2. A profile of Blue 4 Behaviour

In this example, an individual manager's immediate reports' responses are aggregated to show them delivering 45% of their behaviour characterized as being Blue 4. The other quadrants are reported as 25% Red, 5% Amber and 25% Green. From our normative database, this profile highlights some significant deficiencies in the quality of this person's leadership. Their behavioural style is less likely to cultivate a Climate characterized by the Five Cs. We see that a score of 70-75% Blue 4 represents the threshold above which can be expected to emerge a distinctively superior quality of leadership.

In this profile the individual needs to focus developmentally on closing the 20% gap between current and desired level of Blue 4. The relatively high scores for Red and Green are interesting because they seem contradictory; how is it possible to be both a dictator and pacifier? you may ask. Just a short thought gives the answer. How many times have you had a reprimand from your boss in the morning, only to have him pat you on the back in the afternoon and buy you a drink after work? We're being slightly flippant here, but you get the point! (Incidentally, Red and Green don't make Blue.)

In addition to this measure of behavioural style, it is also useful to consider a measure of frequency. In particular, we are looking at the frequency with which a leader exhibits behaviours relating to four contextual situations, namely Direction Setting, Communication, Decision Making and Performance Management. As a result, it is possible to produce a combined report showing the extent to which the leader operates in four critical areas of managerial responsibility and does so (or not) in a Blue 4 style. This is illustrated in Figure 8.3.

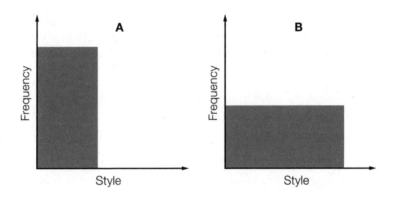

Figure 8.3.: Frequency vs. Style

In illustration A, we see a high frequency (70%) and a low style of Blue 4 (35%). If this data represents the aggregation of a manager's team of direct reports, it is indicating that they consider the manager does a lot of, say, Direction Setting, but not in a Blue 4 style. Depending upon the dominant style, the team could feel coerced (Red), disregarded (Amber) or that the issue is treated with insufficient seriousness (Green). Illustration B shows the opposite with low frequency of Direction Setting (30%) but delivered with strong emphasis of Blue 4 style. In this context, the team may say, "He doesn't do it very often but when he does it is done very effectively."

This quantitative data can be supplemented with qualitative feedback, e.g. from an event-based behavioural interview, coupled with quantitative Climate measurement. This provides a very powerful point of origin to any change initiative. There is a clear sense of where things stand and, as such, a definitive "line in the sand" can be drawn, which represents the start point for any leadership development program designed to bring about an enhanced engagement capability that will result in a stronger Climate for change being established and maintained.

Implementation

We suggest a four-stage development program to raise leadership capability to deliver significant organizational change.

1. Establish a Learning and Development Program in which managers understand the concept of Blue 4 and how it drives Climate and how, in turn, Climate drives performance. This includes benchmark assessment of Behavior/Predisposition/Climate together with the key performance indicators.

2. Provision of a learning environment in which leaders can safely practice the tools and approaches associated with delivering Blue 4 behavioural style.

3. A structured approach for taking the learning back into the workplace for practical application in the context of real life change agenda issues.

4. Track progress and apply measurement of Behaviour, Climate and the key performance indicators.

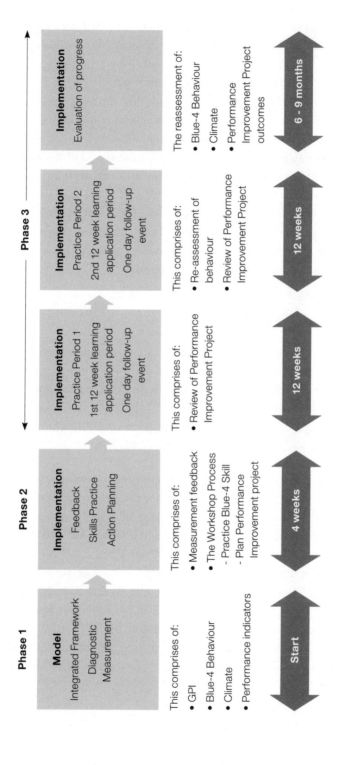

Figure 8.4: The Development Journey

Figure 8.4 outlines our critical execution process, which we call Engagement through Leadership Skills, or ETLS™. Following the formal learning intervention, which can be one-on-one or team-based, participants return to work to apply their newly learned skills on a specific engagement issue that is impeding their progression of change. This approach works as well with the CEO confronting a difficult situation with a fellow board member, be they an executive or non-executive, or a team leader fronting a team of production engineers in a chemical production process. Furthermore, the process can be "industrialized" so that within an organization a team of line managers and HR counterparts can be trained to cascade the concept of Blue 4 skills development across all parts of the enterprise. ETLS™ represents a learning mechanism by which Model, Measure, iMplement can be brought to life in a realistic manner and deliver genuine, positive return on the investment cost of conducting the program.

A Series of Case Studies

The first study involved a financial services organization with a distinctly mediocre track record in terms of operational delivery. The background was a demerger of their international business with this learning implementation involving the residual but significantly sized UK-based national business. At the heart of the new enterprise's strategy lay a commitment to develop operational efficiency.

The start point was a measurement/assessment process incorporating focus group sessions with all of the employees from the new organization. This provided a wealth of qualitative data in terms of what worked well and what didn't work well within the organization as a whole. We also measured the Organizational Climate through quantitative survey. This provided a quantitative benchmark from the employees. The Climate provided a measure in terms of how people felt about the organization in terms of factors such as Clarity, Commitment, etc. Finally, Blue 4 behaviour was measured with the overall management population (there were 60 managers in total). There were also a number of business performance outcome measures collected. This measurement process was conducted at the beginning of 2009.

Based on the data and feedback, which indicated very poor levels of Blue 4 behaviour, Climate and performance, the organization implemented the ETLS™ process described above during the course of 2009. This comprised a series of awareness and feedback workshops, Blue 4 skills development workshops and back at work "case study" improvement projects which in part represented implementations of the learning. The development intervention as a whole was formally completed by the end of 2010.

During 2010 the Climate and Blue 4 behaviours were resurveyed and, in addition, the focus group sessions were all reconvened. Also the full raft of performance indicators taken in 2009 were fully reassessed.

Summary of Results

From the focus groups, a consistent pattern of leadership behaviour and Climate improvement over the course of this time frame were indicated. Many individuals gave quite specific examples of how their leaders had changed and enhanced their delivery. Perhaps more significant are the quantitative results which showed an average of 10% shift in the level of Blue 4 behaviour. This underpinned a 20% shift in the level of Climate. Clarity for example moved from 25% in 2009 to 50% in 2010.

More impressive are the bottom line indicators. These showed a range of improvements: in the call center, to business planning, IT and facilities improvements etc. Debt recovery realized a 17% net improvement. This approach of Model, Measure, iMplement generated a 10% shift in leadership behaviour which in turn underpinned a 20% improvement in Climate. The estimate of bottom line improvement was about 39%. Evidence from the focus groups (2009/10) strongly supported the conclusion that the ETLS™ and Climate interventions were massive drivers of these performance outcomes.

These numbers are not untypical of these types of interventions. Figure 8.5 presents the strapline we sometimes use to convey the quantitative link between Behaviour, Climate and Performance.

- Behaviour/Climate/Performance connections
- 10/20/40
- A 10 percent shift in behaviour drives a 20 percent shift in climate which drives a 40 percent shift in bottom line performance

Figure 8.5 a strap line to the link for performance

These types of quantitative data clearly show impressive results. However, in many respects it is the insights from the focus groups which provide a more powerful and interesting picture of what actually happened. The "Martin story" provides a fabulous anecdote:

The Martin Story

Let's call him Martin, he is a senior manager of 25 years' experience in this business, has a legal background, is quite a serious individual and dedicated to his work. He managed the Debt Recovery Group. In 2009 his Blue 4 score was 39% and associated with poor Climate profiles. In 2010 his Blue 4 score had increased to 57% with highly impressive hikes at the level of Organizational Climate and bottom line performance within his area of accountability. During the second round of focus group meetings there was an opportunity to hear some of the feedback from Martin's immediate reports; one individual said:

"Martin really changed the way he operated as a result of going through the ETLS process. He began to delegate tasks that previously he had kept very close to his chest and this had a significant effect on what we were able to achieve and I guess really lifted the morale of the team. There is no doubt that this change in how we did things really made a difference and I suppose is primarily why we have been able to improve our performance."

These were, of course, quite positive remarks; a rather more mixed comment came from another of Martin's direct reports. She said:

"Well, he only changed because he had to." It was obvious to the facilitator that this individual was not that keen on Martin but the facilitator nevertheless answered by asking, *"But did he actually change and did it have a positive impact on your performance?"* She responded quickly by saying, *"Well I suppose he did change and we are performing better but nevertheless I think he only changed because he had to."*

The facilitator of course did not pursue this any further and I suppose we can look at Martin and his relationship with this individual as being on a development curve where he has at least made a good start. Taken seriously of course it is quite a neat example of the slowness of people's attitudes to change. We can look at this process as an initial development of change behaviour which has delivered solid outcomes and that is great, but we can see that Martin needs to maintain this behavioural style over time in order eventually to shift the deep-held negative attitude portrayed by this particular immediate report. The Martin story as a whole, however, certainly indicates the feasibility of behavioural change and the potential rewards that you can get from it. Four years on, his manager reported that Martin has maintained this shift and that performance in bottom line terms has continued to move upward.

The data results from the Martin story are presented in Figure 8.6 below. These illustrate Martin's predominantly Red and Amber leadership behaviour at the beginning of the development program (time 1) and 9 months later (time 2) we see a significant reduction in Red and Amber and a Blue 4 improvement of 25%. We observed this improvement in behaviour underpinning a substantial shift in the Climate as indicated above with an associated business performance improvement of 17% net in terms of debt recovery.

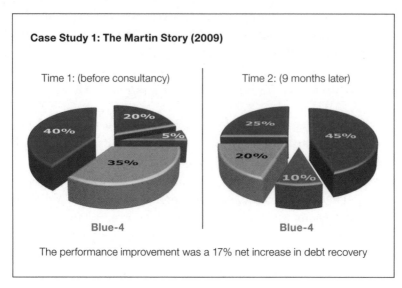

Figure 8.6: The Martin Story

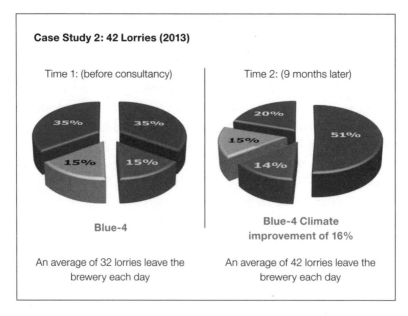

Figure 8.7: 42 Lorries

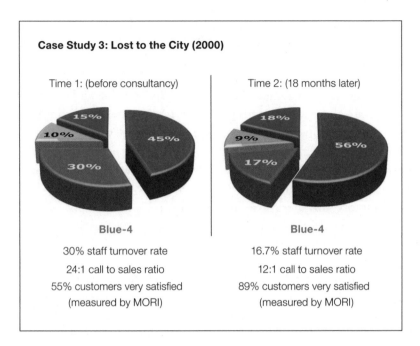

Figure 8.8: Lost to the City (2000)

Two further case studies are illustrated in Figures 8.7 and 8.8 respectively. The first of these is entitled "42 lorries" and the second is entitled "Lost to the City."

The 42 lorries case study focuses on a logistics leader of a major African brewery. The key performance issue was around poor levels of productivity. This situation was an organization with significant production capacity and sales potential; the issue was product distribution. The average number of lorries leaving a brewery each day was 32. The logistics director was highly frustrated with what he perceived to be a very low level of productivity (i.e. number of loaded-up lorries leaving each day) but seemingly unable to get his team to address the issue.

Our analysis indicated that this leader's style was predominantly Red with Climate analysis indicating his team seemed like "rabbits in headlights" with an apparent command and control leadership which inhibited their innovation. Figure 8.7 indicates the substantial change in behaviour which this logistics leader achieved. In summary, he reduced his Red style and enhanced his level of Blue 4 over a nine-month period which had the impact of improving the Climate within the operation which he managed.

The performance improvement at a business level was dramatic with the average of 32 lorries a day moving to 42 lorries a day (i.e. on average leaving each brewery).

The second case study entitled "Lost to the City" involved a London-based (part of a global corporation) pension/asset management company in terms of its call center operation. The initial background was an organization experiencing very high staff turnover together with an expensive recruitment and training process for call center advisors. In fact, the main reason for becoming involved in this work was to stem the flow of call center advisors leaving the organization for more attractive roles in the City of London. Subsequent analysis however also showed fairly mediocre sales performance and customer satisfaction levels.

The key focus of the intervention was to enable the leadership population to enhance its behaviour and culture with a view to achieving improvement in these performance issues. These results are summarized in Figure 8.8. The results show that over an 18-month period the leadership population as a whole improved its level of Blue 4 behaviour from 45% to 56% - on average an improvement of 11% Blue 4. Again, our analysis indicated that this enhancement of Blue (and corresponding decreasing Green) enhanced the Climate and delivered significant improvements in the three key performance indicators. Over this period staff turnover moved from 30% to 16.7%, the call/sales ratio went from 24:1 to 12:1. Finally, 55% of customers "very satisfied" went to 89% of customers "very satisfied" (as measured by MORI).

We argue that any change intervention will require an enhancement in leadership capability in order to secure the opportunity. We further argue that this type of behavioural change is eminently feasible and in the context of a 12-month period you can make real progress. If you drive up leadership delivery you'll manage the Five Cs more effectively, and if you do that you will secure a return on investment. By the way, when we use the term ROI we do not mean the cost of the training because the cost of the training is minimal. We mean a return on investment in terms of the overall change program. These examples are three of many that can be cited. The achievements indicated are highly feasible, the key point is whether you as leader or group of leaders in a changed context believe it and want to do it. Our final comment is this: well do you?

CHAPTER 9

Getting people on board – the role of Influencing

In an earlier chapter, we made the point that we see many change initiatives being led by a senior manager who still needs to gain support by means of emphasizing the fact that their initiative is being "sponsored" by the CEO, or other senior executive. This approach never quite achieves what people expect and thus it should be used sparingly and only as part of an influencing approach not as an alternative! Instead, whoever leads the change needs to create a Climate that is built through astute and adept influencing, drawing significantly on the attributes of Blue 4 behaviour described earlier.

While some change leaders Influence almost intuitively, for the rest of us this behaviour doesn't come naturally. So, in this chapter we want to set out our behavioural approach to efficient and effective influencing.

Without equivocation, the ability to influence effectively is central and pivotal to the success of any change intervention.

We look at influencing in terms of a process. We use as our lens to coordinate our engagement and influencing approach a framework we call the Influencing Model (Figure 9.1). The model encompasses three areas of activity that are central to effective change and which entirely map on to the high-level structure of a behavioural competency framework. The three areas are Visioning, Networking and Realization.

Any successful change agenda firstly needs to be underpinned by a clear sense of what the leader wants to achieve. In terms of the model, we refer to this process as "the vision." Whatever the vision might be, without getting other people on board it has no chance of success. (Incidentally, this applies to a personal vision as much as a corporate one; for instance, the individual who decides they want to run a marathon having not done anything like that before needs to gain the support and encouragement of family and friends). The organizational stakeholders, or perhaps a better term is the leader's network, is critical to the success of the change process. Such individuals may well sit within the more immediate sphere of the leader or they may represent external entities outside of the organization, e.g. opinion formers such as politicians, journalists, lobby groups, and others operating with its service-profit chain from up-stream suppliers to down-stream service support. In short, the network consists of any individual or group of individuals that can impact or influence the success of the vision. In this sense, therefore, we define the second component of the change process as networking.

Getting visioning and networking right is critical, but referring back to the new CEO one of the authors worked with, ultimately something has to happen. Richard Branson is quoted as saying that nothing happens in business until something is sold; change needs to be sold. From the grandiose ideas and networking, a favorable result must emerge. The third critical element of the change process is realization. Put more specifically, what we are talking about here concerns the things a leader needs to do and the activities that need to happen in order for them to realize the outcome of their initial vision.

	Vision	Network	Realisation
Vision	① Has an idea for change	② Thinks through the full network process	③ Thinks through and plans all the activities that need to be done
Network	④ Test out the idea with significant others	⑤ Fully engages the network	⑥ Engages with people to get the work done
Realisation	⑦ Works up a high level plan	⑧ Secures the commitment of the network	⑨ Evaluates/monitors the quality of the work done

Fig 9.1: The Influencing Model

Combining these three components produces the matrix shown in Figure 9.1. Both horizontally and vertically, we show the three domains of Visioning, Networking and Realization. One reads the matrix down the first column, then down the second and, finally, down the third. The roadmap (to adopt the term from the preceding chapter) encompasses steps of Visioning the Vision (cell 1), Networking the Vision (cell 2) and so on through Networking the Network (cell 5) and on to Realizing the Realization (cell 9). The matrix is a simplified abstraction of a well-managed change process. Let's go through each of the steps of this nine-box Influencing Model.

Rather than remain in an abstract or conceptual world, let us use a practical real life event to add some shape and color to what these nine steps actually mean. The example we use is a relatively simple account of how one of our colleagues managed to purchase a derelict barn and convert it into a beautiful family home.

We will call this the "Simon story." Simon is a 40-year-old bachelor who is about to marry and start a family. High on the couple's agenda is the need to acquire a family home in which to live and raise a family.

1 - Visioning the Vision

One summer afternoon when Simon is driving home from work he notices a For Sale sign sticking out of the hedge alongside the country lane along which he is driving. Simon immediately stops the car and decides to have a look around. He walks up the pathway and there in front of him is a broken-down and derelict old barn. Simon is filled with great excitement at this point. He envisages something in the future. The barn is converted into a pristine, comfortable property that is home for him, his partner and their future children. It will be a sensational place to live and bring up a family, meeting his values and aspirations. Simon has an idea of what could be achieved but, literally, at this stage it is no more than a thought in his own mind. From a competency or behaviour point of view this involves Conceptual Thinking in the main. One could also construe that in thinking about his partner's needs, he has applied some Interpersonal Awareness. Simon needs to step into the second cell.

2 – Networking the Vision

This concerns Simon testing out his idea with significant others, i.e. his partner.

Upon getting home, Simon immediately begins the process of testing out his idea with her. What does she think? Is it a good idea? Consciously, deliberately, Simon "positions" the origin of the idea as lying in a suggestion she had made when talking about ideal places to live and considering a barn conversion (albeit a completed one rather than one they would manage themselves).

"You remember the other week when you were talking about Barry's barn conversion and how you thought we should look to see if any are on the market, well I drove home down the lanes this evening and saw this For Sale sign sticking out the hedge…" This style of engagement is to get his partner "on board." It is certainly not indifferent by virtue of showing concern to praise his partner's original train of thought. It is also not passive because Simon surfaces the issues of how the benefits, i.e. a luxurious property in a rural situation that won't cost the earth, outweigh the undoubted challenge of managing the conversion process themselves. Simon "strokes" his partner's ego by saying how much she rises to a challenge. Furthermore, Simon is at pains to outline to her some of the practical steps he has identified that they need to undertake to get the project rolling. Simon's interaction is therefore a neat piece of Blue 4.

Another part of the activities within cell 2 involves Simon speaking to people within his network who he knows have some knowledge about converting barns. This network is in place, it doesn't need to be built. It is both physical and virtual. A colleague in a factory plant elsewhere in the country lives in a barn conversion. Following his partner's initial suggestion, Simon has found a discussion group on the internet and has been chatting to them intermittently for the past month gathering information. His brother's best friend is a quantity surveyor, which is slightly serendipitous but these things happen. Simon tells his partner he is going to engage with these people and does so. The result is a great deal of encouragement from everyone with some clear steps about what Simon needs to do next. Simon and his partner share what they have discovered, which provides clarity about what needs to be done next.

Behaviourally, he is thinking ahead, so Forward Thinking is being applied. As he moves from broad-based Conceptual Thinking, he is thinking a little more logically and rationally, so Analytical Thinking is being utilized. What is certainly coming to the fore in cell 2 is the relationship building.

3 – Realizing the Vision

Success in cell 2 means that Simon has achieved two critical outcomes: firstly through sharing his idea with his partner in the manner he did he gained her enthusiastic buy-in; and secondly he gained information from his network that helped him "polish" his idea and determine what he needed to do next. It all helped establish the feasibility of the original idea from cell 1 and therefore enable movement into the next stage.

Cell 3 is about producing a plan that is sufficiently detailed in setting out the steps that now need to be taken. What Simon does now is to establish a high-level plan about *what* he needs to do and the critical steps that need to be taken. This enables Simon to move into what is probably the critical column of networking.

In this cell, the thinking is more literal and linear, i.e. what needs to be done. So, Analytical Thinking combined with Forward Thinking. Initiative is needed as is Critical Information Seeking, i.e. why is the barn priced so favorably? What are all the outbuildings used for on the neighboring land?

4 - Visioning the Network

Here Simon takes considerable time to think through (with his partner's help) who he needs to talk to, about what, why, by when and how, i.e. which is the best media to use. This is Simon's "stakeholder map" or "networking web."

Simon is attempting to identify all those individuals that might be impacted or affected by the project or, in some way, can either help or hinder his ambitions. Simon implicitly understands the Change Equation; he knows he will face resistance from some, e.g. neighbors to the barn who may object to the planning application, and he has to think through the benefits they will gain from him converting the barn. He knows he is going to have to negotiate a purchase price and fees with contractors and professional service providers. He knows he is going to confront bureaucracy and officialdom. For each "node on the network", which is impersonal admittedly but, as yet, he doesn't know who he will be engaging with, he works out his approach and how he will manage probable objections. He begins to sketch out his thoughts about the layout of the barn after conversion and shares these with his partner.

Here Simon is applying Strategic Influencing behaviour across his network which, as mentioned, has been deliberately put in place by his strength of Relationship Building. The network is approached in such a way that mutual benefit is readily identified; this is not a time for being belligerent.

This fourth cell is a very major step and demands significant effort. In many instances someone is overlooked, which creates subsequent problems although usually and fortunately not catastrophic. Despite the criticality of this step, we encounter so many organizational change initiatives that ignore and bypass cells 2 to 4 and commence in cell 5.

5 – Networking the Network

Here Simon is actually going to engage with his network. However, this is not a blundering, half-cocked approach because he has identified during cell 4 who he is going to engage with, about what, why, when, how, where. Many decades ago Rudyard Kipling wrote: "I keep six honest serving men, They taught me all I knew, Their names are What and Why and When and How and Where and Who." It remains entirely apposite to effective networking.

In each engagement he will make sure he positions his arguments and explanations of his needs carefully, in the right way, and that he raises the right issue with the relevant person. He has thought about the other person's needs and expectations; he has managed his composure and demeanor, his own behaviours. He has applied Emotional Intelligence but, critically, has done so by explicitly considering both facets, i.e. Interpersonal Awareness *and* Concern for Impact. As we mentioned earlier, Emotional Intelligence is the convergence of these two discrete and additive behaviours. If you wish, Interpersonal Awareness is your mental radar screen: who's out there, what are they doing and why? Concern for Impact is using that information to positive effect, e.g. John is all about detail, Sandra is high-level, so that's what they're served.

In practical terms, Simon's process involves meetings with the local authority's planning department, meeting up with financial providers, it means talking to local builders and getting quotes. If you like, he runs the beauty parade of suppliers and is clear with them about what he expects and when he wants the work to start and to be completed.

Here, ongoing Strategic Influencing pulls on the crucial aspect of Relationship Building, i.e. seeking the win-win, and tactically behaving adroitly through subtle application of Interpersonal Awareness and Concern for Impact, the wheels begin to turn. The self-managing behaviours also play out in terms of Tenacity and Flexibility.

6 – Realizing the Network

It's great for people to be well connected or networked; for some, it's an ego trip to have a big social network. However, it is of absolutely no use whatsoever if that group of people cannot be brought on board in terms of what the "visioner" wants to achieve. Securing involvement and commitment from the network is essential. It is at this point that Simon's behavioural characteristics move from thinking and influencing to achieving outcomes. In practical terms, this means he gains planning permission, he obtains the necessary finance from the banks, he appoints an architect, and he employs a builder whom he trusts to subcontract capable tradesmen, and they agree to do the job.

Here, the crucial combination of behaviours is further application of Relationship Building augmented by Independence and Results Focus, i.e. asking for and securing the loan, asking the contractor to do the work and securing their agreement, also with Concern for Impact, agreeing mutually favorable deals.

7 – Visioning the Realization

Simon now enters the realization column of the Influencing model. At this stage of Simon's change process he has successfully gained initial commitment from significant others to his idea and entirely brought his full network on board such that commitment of all the stakeholders to the project has been secured. Simon is now ready to press the green button for action which is what the realization phase of the change process is all about.

In cell 7, Simon starts the process of visioning his realization process. This is to do with thinking through all of the activities that need to happen in order to deliver his barn conversion. It is in fact the detailed planning process, which he may or may not do personally. Simon needs to establish clearly a project plan and identify all the critical steps and objectives that need to be undertaken. It paves the way for cell 8 which is when the real work gets going.

Behaviourally, we see the planning demand use of Analytical and Forward Thinking. It is quite possible that throughout the majority of these stages, Simon has been objectively learning new things, so Self-development has not been overlooked.

8 – Networking the Realization

Simon has all the pieces in place, the network is on board, action is underway, building has commenced. Simon now needs to keep in touch with all the people involved in bringing his vision to fruition; literally, he needs to manage his relationships in a mutually beneficial manner. He needs to remind them of his expectations for quality and timeliness without being too domineering. Taking the building crew on a wet Friday morning in late winter off-site for a cooked breakfast will do no harm whatsoever! Visiting the site to coincide with timely completion of key stages to say thanks is constructive. Being supportive when reviewing plans that have been upended by unforeseen circumstances, e.g. appalling weather, the failure of a supplier, but without being overtly accepting (passive) is important.

These are simplistic examples but make the point (and from our own awareness engaging with colleagues and clients similar to Simon, they work!). The behaviours that Simon needs to deliver in cell 8 are critical and not dissimilar to those we indicate are needed in cell 5. It is all about the manner in which he engages with those other people who, at this stage, are more crucial to delivering the vision than he is. Simon must be appropriately Directional and Engaging – he must be Blue 4. Being Red 1 will simply antagonize; Amber 2 will see issues avoided and Green 3 will see issues made light of. In the more atomistic sense of individual competencies, Simon needs to show his Interpersonal Awareness and Concern for Impact but must also demonstrate Concern for Excellence, Independence, Flexibility, Tenacity and Results Focus.

9 – Realizing the Realization

We now come to the final part of the process which is cell 9. The work is done and it's time for Simon to actually evaluate how the work has gone. Does it meet the standard? Does any more work need to be redone or reworked? It's about performance management in terms of evaluation of the outcomes. Here the Results Focus and Concern for Excellence behaviours concerns evaluation and learning, and Independence with Concern for Impact enables this learning to be shared with his team. This is a crucial stage of the process. Without it, in an organizational sense, no organization can hope to become a "learning organization."

The Influencing Model is a simple framework that helps to articulate the different types of behaviours that leaders need to do in order to make change happen. From the initial vision or idea comes a series of requirements that the successful change leader needs to adopt if they are going to be successful. It is of course an oversimplification because change programs of any type will be entirely iterative and not simply linear movements in terms of nine stages or the cells of this matrix. The model simply serves to illustrate the different aspects of a change program that need to be delivered and how different types of behaviours become more or less important at each stage. It also emphasizes the criticality of the influencing, networking or engaging process; bear in mind that fully two-thirds of this Influencing Model are traversed before even one brick gets laid.

The first three boxes are predominantly under the visioning label and there will be a requirement in terms of the thinking skills of the change leader: having the idea in the first place. These thinking skills are clearly supported by important influencing and delivery behaviours. The initial idea of course would be dead in the water if Simon didn't have the wit to present it to his partner in the right way and thus get that initial support.

The Networking column is fundamentally the people dimension. Different aspects of influencing are underpinned by certain characteristics. For example, cell 4 will have a high degree of thinking very carefully about the constitution of the network and how best to approach those folk to bring them on board, fully committed to what needs to be done in what time frame. On the other hand, cell 5 represents the "full on" engagement process, which is when the change leader actually needs to interact with others and, as mentioned, Emotional Intelligence comes to the fore. Finally, cell 6 secures people's agreement to action; things can start to happen.

Within the narrative of this story, we have deliberately woven in references to the particular behaviours we see as most important within each stage of the process. These behaviours are very much the "atoms" of the overall approach that needs to be taken, which is, throughout, that of being Blue 4. Purpose, pace, energy, objectivity corroborate with the necessary level of being Directive rather than Passive. Ensuring people are on board and feel included, dealing with issues sensibly and calmly, shows Concern rather than Indifference. Blue 4 gets the job, in this case, Simon's barn conversion, completed on time, to budget and to superb quality. The wedding isn't interrupted by the workmen still fitting the kitchen! Everyone involved, especially the tradesmen, gets a great reference from Simon. They win more business.

Influencing Behaviours

Our referencing of behaviours has been somewhat light-touch, so let us take some time to explain in more detail what we are actually talking about.

The four specific influencing behaviours that Simon used were Strategic Influencing, Relationship Building, Interpersonal Awareness and Concern for Impact.

We have interviewed thousands of senior executives and other organizational leaders from across the world in every sector ranging from the purpose of recruitment and selection to development in terms of talent management and succession planning. Influencing is so crucial to things happening well, yet we have found is generally done poorly. The "gung-ho" aggression portrayed in drama, soaps, and reality TV *may* make good entertainment but it does not work in the long run of organizational life. Consider some of the comments made about the leaders of the failed financial institutions. Their aggressive behavioural style didn't pay off - either for them or the wider geo-economic world. Fast proved to be the old slow. Influencing is entirely about making slow the new fast!

Strategic Influencing

Based on their idea/vision for change, an individual thinks through how to create and conduct a successful, positively engaging influencing strategy with stakeholders inside and outside their organization.

"Mark saw himself as a leader of change and I can remember when he joined us that he had a clear view about what needed to change and improve over the course of the next few years. The key point, however, was that he really applied a broad range of influencing tactics and styles to bring all the various parties on board to his view of things. He was no 'one trick pony' in terms of the manner in which he engaged with all the different people. In so doing, he won the commitment of these people to his long-term objectives."

Mark demonstrates his ability as a strategic influencer by first of all having a view about what needs to change in the medium to longer term, i.e. beyond two to three years. He recognized that the need to get people on board would only be achieved by deploying a range of different influencing tactics in order to build commitment.

Relationship Building

Over the long-term, an individual builds a network of contacts which can be mutually beneficial to their respective business activities.

"I don't think I ever met anyone so well connected as Mary. She seemed to know such a wide range of people, not only from her direct experience in terms of roles that she'd occupied but also much broader at both an industry and external level. There is no doubt that if you ever wanted some advice about who to go and see then Mary could always tell you who the key players were and she was always able to give you an introduction. I do know that while Mary worked very hard in terms of her main role she always made time over the years to build and maintain a great set of contacts."

Mary demonstrates her ability as a relationship builder because she puts time and effort into making contact with people and developing a relationship with them where the task requirements are not the key driver. She has simply built up a broad network of contacts which enables her whenever relevant to seek input and help from that network over the long-term.

Interpersonal Awareness

An individual thinks carefully to understand what drives and motivates other people.

"The person to go and ask about how the land lies is definitely Richard. He just seems to have a very good handle on what makes folk tick. The other week I had a conversation with him about one of our colleagues in the sales department. It was so useful to hear his insight about the person in question that I saw that person in a different light regarding their probable ulterior motives."

Richard shows his interpersonal awareness by providing to his colleague a really useful insight about the concerns, drivers and motives of another person.

Concern for Impact

An individual actively modifies their behaviours with others in order to engage with them effectively in order to win their buy-in.

"Sometimes I am amazed with Jane's skill in getting people to see things her way. Last year she made a presentation to the engineering department about the need for them to align their activities carefully in terms of the organization's marketing and sales activities. When she presented her argument she described it in such a way using facts and figures that it seemed to really appeal to those guys. She absolutely got them on board by how she made her input."

Jane demonstrates her concern for impact by positioning her argument in a certain way that captured the imagination of the engineers and got them to do what the business required.

To strengthen our earlier remark about recognizing the bi-dimensional nature of Emotional Intelligence, it is worth mentioning that we have met people who abound in Interpersonal Awareness but possess little or no Concern for Impact. They can peer into a meeting room and immediately read the body language and subtle non-verbal communication signals occurring. Yet, if they go into the room, indeed any room, they are singular in their approach. Conversely, we meet people who can describe vividly how they behaved in a certain manner in one situation but very differently in another yet can't elucidate why; so, little Interpersonal Awareness but bags of Concern for Impact. Over time, their overall behavioural quality of Influencing will not be as good as is the case for the individual who combines strength in both behaviours.

One other point to make is that we see behavioural frameworks containing dozens of behaviours, perhaps 20 relating to Influencing. Firstly, we remain dubious that many of these are actually behaviours. For instance, Change Management is not a behaviour! It is a process. Leadership is certainly not a behaviour. It is, however, an outcome of behaviours; either it prevails due to behaviour or doesn't.

Secondly, the effectiveness of a behavioural framework is not judged by the number of behaviours it contains. The human mind is finite in its capacity to process concurrent trains of mental cognition. Frameworks we have designed have, on average, 20 behaviours overall. The human brain can cope with this. People don't feel blinded by science. Such a framework is valid and practical.

How these Behaviours link to Change

Our work shows that successful influencers of change deliver the end-to-end change process through the appropriate and effective use of four critical influencing behaviours. Let's consider how each of these behaviours relate and indeed underpin each element of the Influencing Model we described earlier.

Strategic Influencing

This behaviour is the most fundamental to any change program. In many respects, it represents an elegant choreography of an influencing process. Firstly, the change leader has an idea about what they want to change in their organization, why they want to do this and what benefits will accrue to it as an entity and the people involved with it, be they investors, trustees, suppliers, customers or employees. This is the "acorn" of the change process, which needs to be sown and nurtured.

In the context of the example concerning Simon, his change agenda related to his and his partner's entire set of values and aspirations in terms of their lifestyle as a married couple and parents.

In a large corporation, we are more concerned with the fundamentals of its culture and how things are done and, thereby, how people will feel, i.e.

the overall Organizational Climate. Given this perspective, the effective Strategic Influencer will think comprehensively through the way in which all the relevant "actors" in the network need to be engaged with. They will have considered who are the really key players, their roles, who they engage with, their aims and ambitions, what "strokes" they respond to favorably (this is not to countenance inducement, of course, but for some folks their status is important, for others they want to be respected for their range or depth of knowledge). Crucial is the way each "actor" is viewed against the Change Equation. What will they respond to that lowers their resistance to the proposed change?

The Strategic Influencer will think through a series of tactics about how things need to be positioned and how the overall engagement process will be conducted, e.g. what to say to whom, how to say it to them, which communication channel to use, e.g. Skype or convivial dinner, time and place, etc.

This is indeed complex choreography. If not thought through effectively, the actors, dancers and acrobats crash into each other and the show is a failure. In change, the initiative careers off the rails.

Remember the Change Equation states that individuals impacted by change need to perceive that the benefit to them will outweigh the pain to them and that it's worth it to them.

Crudely put, people don't do things that aren't in their interests. What gains engagement is, of course, Clarity about what is going to happen and why.

In terms of the nine-box model it is probably Strategic Influencing behaviour that really underpins cells 2, 4 and 5. Cell 2 is "light touch" as Simon needs to bring the key player, i.e. his partner, on board. However, if his or her parents were making a contribution to the purchase of the marital home, they too would have needed to be engaged. In cells 4 and 5, we find a greater demand for the behaviour as there is a wider variation of types of actor to which Simon needs to give consideration. These include a whole range of suppliers from banks to builders to planning authority to the farmer selling the barn, etc. Simon was required to consider these people in depth and work out how he should proceed in terms of their engagement. Cells 5 and 6 are the implementation of that network thinking. We shall see in a moment other additional behaviours that need to be brought to the mix.

Applying this choreography to the broader corporate context, where a change leader appointed by the CEO to manage, say, a demerger, Strategic Influencing is the far more effective way to achieve a clean and successful split for both enterprises rather than clumsily wielding the hammer of "sponsorship." "Bob has told me to get this sorted" tends to get people's backs up.

Of course, this is a far more complex and intense influencing challenge than Simon faced, but at heart it requires the same cognitive approach in order to address the crux of the problem posed by the Change Equation. Strategic Influencing is a fundamental differentiator between outstanding and average leadership performance in a change context yet we see it is a scarce commodity. Strategic Influencing does not just concern the "what" of a vision, i.e. to double TSR in three years. It much more concerns the "how." What is needed to make that vision reality? What resources are required? How are they obtained? How do they need to be marshaled once acquired to deliver the vision? Visioning has become a one-dimensional commodity evinced by posters on the wall and website home pages. It is so much more than that.

Strategic Influencing takes the strategic thinking out to those who will be involved and/or affected by the change. It is the lever that will overcome resistance – if not all of it, most of it. In so achieving this, it highlights what needs to be done with the stubborn and unyielding. Contingencies can be considered and suggested.

As remarked, Strategic Influencing is not a well-developed, frequently observed behaviour. Perhaps by virtue of social pressure, the favored way is that of coercion and rational persuasion. The numbers may look good but the epithet attached to accountants, i.e. they count beans but can't explain their nutritional value, rings true. Organizations are defined as groups of people brought together to achieve a common aim. Influencing is entirely people orientated. The bottom line of such is that if any member of the network does not perceive a benefit to them and does not understand clearly what the first key steps are, then at best they won't be motivated to put in effort, at worst they'll engage in downright sabotage.

Relationship Building

By relationship building we do not mean just the act of having good relationships with others, although this is crucial. What we mean is the idea of a change leader practicing a long-term networking approach. This causes them to build contacts with people they can readily approach and seek support from. This is bilateral, by the way.

Great relationship builders build relationships for their own sakes and usage in the future for mutual benefit. Relationships are not just acquired in order to complete a particular task or project. The key questions to ask any individual who aspires to be a relationship builder are these:

- Do you spend time building relationships outside of the context of your immediate task requirements with a view that those relationship contacts may/will have some value in the future?

- Do you continue to maintain and nurture those relationships over time?

- Do you think about which external groups you should engage for the future?

- Do you consider how you may add value to others outside of your immediate contacts and current task activities?

The key point about relationship building is that the work has already been done. In other words, the network that the change leader is using has been established in the past and it is something that they call on when required.

In the context of Simon's barn conversion, he had a network, both physical and virtual, that he was able to engage with straight away upon seeing the dilapidated barn. There was no out-of-the-blue call to someone he didn't know, stultified by introductions and explaining who he was and what he wanted. He was able to make contact and seek advice.

Additionally to what we relayed when telling the story, Simon had forged relationships in the local community. He knew someone who knew the farmer selling the barn. An introduction was effected and dialogue commenced.

In this example of everyday local life, Simon is a person who is well connected and this connection or connectedness was no accident. He is the sort of person who does Relationship Building. It put him in a position where he could call on contacts for support.

In the more complex corporate environment, the socially powerful change leader will similarly have built such a wealth of contacts through their effective Relationship Building. They are, of course, not just contacts, they are genuine relationships which prevail throughout the organization in which they operate as well as externally. They provide the change leader with a massive advantage in terms of gaining support for their change agenda. In terms of our Influencing model, Relationship Building capability sits alongside Strategic Influencing behaviour within cells 2, 4, 5, 6 and 8.

These two influencing behaviours are high-level and strategic. While they are critically important to the choreography of managing change, they clearly need to be supported by a high degree of Emotional Intelligence, which in our behavioural framework means Interpersonal Awareness and Concern for Impact.

Interpersonal Awareness

Interpersonal Awareness concerns the extent to which the change leader possesses a rich and deep understanding of the needs, motives, concerns and drivers of others. They will undoubtedly acquire a lot of information about others but they will also have a natural tendency to retain this information and reflect on why people do what they do. Ask yourself the following questions in terms of your thought processes:

- Before going to a meeting do you spend most of your time reflecting about the interests and concerns of those that you are meeting with?

- Do you find yourself remembering information about others?

- Do you tend to know stuff about other people's circumstances?

- When you're in meetings do you notice other people's non-verbal behaviour? (Quite often there are cliques within meetings and little nods and winks pass between them as they "politically" steer the meeting toward their ulterior motives. Do you notice these?)

- Following a meeting do you find yourself reflecting on what people said and were, therefore, potentially thinking?

Interpersonally aware individuals notice and reflect upon the actions of others and use that information automatically in the future. They are very good at reading and understanding the meaning of non-verbal behaviour and give considerable thought to the implications of what that might mean. Interpersonally aware individuals spend a lot of time thinking about others. Here we do not necessarily mean caring or being considerate, although from a values point of view this is clearly a positive attribute. We simply mean the concept from a non value-laden perspective.

From a practical point of view, Interpersonal Awareness enables a change leader to enhance the quality of their Concern for Impact delivery. However, as mentioned earlier, these behaviours are discrete so one may be held strongly and the other more weakly. Where both are held in strength, the quality of influencing is magnified considerably. Their EQ, i.e. their Emotional Intelligence quotient (defined in particular behavioural terms of course), is markedly higher.

We have been asked which behaviour is the more important and which should be developed first. Concern for Impact is more visible but how it is perceived by others, to a degree, depends on their proficiency in Interpersonal Awareness. There is a degree of "chicken and egg" here. In the end, we would tend to favor developing Interpersonal Awareness first because in understanding people better you can then learn to adjust your behaviour appropriately.

In terms of our Simon case study, we see his Interpersonal Awareness coming to bear at numerous points in his barn conversion change process. Firstly, his understanding of the concerns and drivers of his partner, where that understanding then helps mold and direct his engagement process. Secondly, we can see how useful that Interpersonal Awareness capability can be throughout cells 4, 5 and 6. It will be particularly powerful in helping him think through his style of influencing approach in cell 4. As we will now go on to see, it underpins how he operates, i.e. his Concern for Impact, in cell 5. Later on, when engaging with the contractors on site, Simon gets his engagement behaviour spot-on.

Concern for Impact

What we mean by Concern for Impact is the individual's ability to adapt and tailor their individual approach to others. For example, the commercial manager who makes a presentation to his operational and engineering colleagues will be highly advised to position and marshall his argument in a way that extols the virtue of efficiency and effectiveness. The argument is likely to be underpinned with a sound set of data and evidence that the intervention can have real practical value. This type of argument is well tailored to this particular population and is likely to be far more effective than an argument that is essentially conceptual and innovative in style.

The savvy (and, in many ways, that is what Concern for Impact concerns) commercial manager will adopt this approach because it is the one which is most likely to appeal to his colleagues. Having Concern for Impact is the ability to deliver the right type of behaviour to win people's support. (This is not about being disingenuous, however; that is poor Concern for Impact and will quickly be perceived by those with strong Interpersonal Awareness.)

Simon realized that to get his partner on board he had to brush her ego by referring back to her initial suggestion to consider barn conversions. Similarly, when making his case to his bank, he needed to have the right impact such that his lender felt the transaction fell within acceptable risk guidelines, otherwise the prospect of getting a loan would be jeopardized.

Simon was adapting his behaviour in order to get the input he required; and even though he considered his idea was a "no brainer", nevertheless he realized that he had to present it in a way that would be in an accord with the values, motives and needs of the other people with whom he was engaging. Indeed, central to his thinking in cells 4 and 5 was a deep consideration of how his total package needed to be presented and positioned with his network. In cell 4 he thought it through and in cell 5 he carried it through in terms of his engagement style.

In cell 8 we saw Simon engaging in the management of the work itself, having sufficient meetings with his building manager so he knew Simon was "on the ball" and keeping track of things but not being so intrusive that the builder felt distrusted. Such style of engagement may not be Simon's natural preference; he may well have preferred to keep his distance. In this situation, however, he recognized he had to maintain a regular discourse with the builder. Taking the team for breakfast one morning was a delightful coup de grâce. This wasn't benevolence or altruism; he knew it was a way of retaining the commitment of the builders to do what they could despite the lousy weather. Self-interest to get the project completed on time rather than kindness drove his behaviour. (In this sense, too, Concern for Impact rests at the heart of the broader Blue 4 engagement style, i.e. Simon's directiveness to keep work moving and concern to keep the builders on side and, thereby, working despite the conditions.) It's a piece of Concern for Impact with Results Focus in mind.

At the corporate level, how a change leader molds and modifies their behaviour with others is absolutely crucial. Its style, content and color will fundamentally impact how people receive messages. Concern for Impact is about both the content and the style of delivery. What you say, how you say it, when you say it and to whom you say it are all absolutely fundamental. (Within the "what", raising the difficult sensitive issue is driven by Independence behaviour; Concern for Impact enables the message to be aired in a way that won't raise hackles.) Engagement lacking in Concern for Impact results in disengagement and failure to influence. The recipient won't see how the change benefits them and, thereby, overcome their resistance. Rather than gain support, poor Concern for Impact can generate antagonism and see resistance grow. Get this wrong and you disengage the recipients of your message.

Strength in both Interpersonal Awareness and Concern for Impact strengthen the ability to deliver the strategic behaviours of Strategic Influencing and Relationship Building. People will feel they are being drawn into something positive and not being manipulated. Where, however, such behaviours are used in a more Machiavellian way, once people realize, all sense of trust and respect flies out the window.

Summary

The whole process of stakeholder management in any change process is absolutely fundamental and it is often the reason why most change programs fail. As we said earlier, at best change programs tend to start at cell 5, wading in and talking to various folk in a somewhat indiscriminate manner. The skilled influencer will combine these four behaviours to deliver effective influencing. Climate will be bolstered because people will possess Clarity and will give their Commitment by virtue of their dancing the two-step choreography of Consistency and Constancy.

CHAPTER 10

Putting it all together

Having made it to the final chapter we feel we owe you a few pages that try to integrate all that you have read. In a way this is no small task in itself given that what precedes this is the result of the authors' collective change management experience and a hefty dollop of the theory that we think makes blinding common sense. So, let us weave together the all-important issues of required behaviours and crucial process steps that need to be undertaken to see through a successful change initiative.

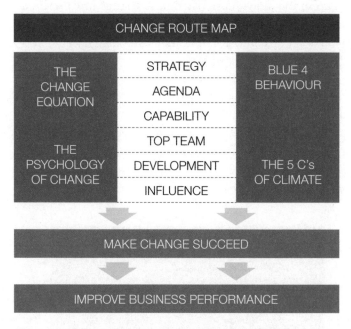

Figure 10.1: A Route Map to enable successful change implementation

In the Introduction we referred to the Route Map Framework which is shown again in Figure 10.1. Central to this was the point that most change programs fail to deliver their promise and there is plenty of evidence to support this view. The obvious question to ask is why these change programs fail and through Chapters 1 to 3 we provided a detailed account of why, from a psychological point of view, this is almost inevitable.

Firstly, change is difficult for the individual. It is a reality of life that people don't want to change unless it is in their interest to do so. We described Festinger's (1957) concept of Cognitive Dissonance. This essentially says that when you try to get people to behave in a way which they don't believe in they will essentially do the behaviour for a short period and then revert to type. In essence you need to find a way to help people persist with the change behaviour because if they do, and if the experience is positive, then in order to overcome their dissonance, their attitudes and beliefs will change in order to embrace the new way of doing things. This theory turns on its head the much-vaunted mantra "We have to capture their hearts and minds." Rather than capturing hearts and minds first, the clear point here is that you need to change behaviour first (of the change followers) with hearts and minds coming later - this is absolutely fundamental.

All bound up in the individual's reaction to change are a series of complex psychological issues relating to differences in personality and motivations which if you don't take into account, then as a change leader you will fail to get people on board with your ideas.

As a way of embracing further this psychology of change, we introduced the Change Equation. This states that in order to get people to change you need to ensure that their dissatisfaction with the current state plus the possession of a clear vision for the future and clarity about the next steps they need to take all need to be stronger than the pain of change. This Change Equation is depicted in Figure 10.2 below.

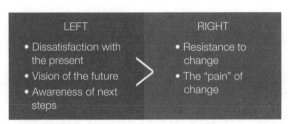

Figure 10.2: The Change Equation

The psychological factors of Predisposition and Motivation are critical elements in how people "engage" in the Change Equation. In terms of Predisposition we describe the idea of an individual's natural or preferred approach and this will influence their perceptions of the upsides or downsides of the proposed change intervention. In particular we cited the Predisposition concept of Radical versus Incremental with Radical types preferring bigger change and Incremental types preferring more step-by-step change. Given that most change consultants (and indeed change leaders) tend to be more Radical than change followers, it is easy to see how conflicts or misunderstandings may occur; at an unconscious level these groups see the world differently. Furthermore, taking the other elements of Predisposition (which were described in Chapter 3) into account makes this even more complex.

Also, in terms of the Motivation theories we saw how different elements of an individual's motive profile may influence how a change situation might appeal or repel. Motives are of course within the individual and if a particular change situation does not match or link or fit with an individual's deep motive drivers then there will be significant implications for the extent to which a change follower may be prepared to stick with the Change Equation. In other words, the motivation of an individual strongly influences whether the left-hand side of the Change Equation exceeds the right-hand side. If these elements of Predisposition and Motivation are managed effectively by the change leader then we have a practical means by which change leaders can enable their change followers to engage in a way which enables sustainable behavioural and attitudinal change to emerge.

In Chapters 1 to 3 we also introduced what it is that makes the difference between successful and unsuccessful change interventions – i.e. whether you succeed in achieving the aims of the Change Equation and therefore achieve sustainable change. The essence of our argument is the critical need to establish the conditions for change. We referred to the Five Cs of Climate which are Clarity, Commitment, Consistency, Constancy and Capability. We defined these Climate dimensions as representing what it feels like to work in an organization and furthermore we position these as the necessary requirements which need to prevail in order to help people through a change program. In essence, the better the Climate then the greater success you will have in enabling people to embrace the change fully.

We also described that the practical way to achieve these Climate conditions is through the behaviour that change leaders actually do. In this context we utilize the idea of Blue 4 behaviour. This is essentially behaviour from a change leader which combines an appropriate balance of direction and concern or focus on people. The change leader will only be successful if they adopt a style of behaviour which is Blue 4 in order to create the right conditions, i.e. Climate for the change. So, the delivery of Blue 4 behaviour creates the Five Cs of Climate which will enable the realization of sustainable, attitudinal and behavioural change with the change followers.

The route map indicates six critical themes that the change leader needs to deliver and which represent or are manifestations of Blue 4 behaviour and therefore the creation of the Five Cs of Climate. The six themes in the framework are:

- Strategy

- Agenda

- Capability

- Top Team

- Development

- Influence

The first of these is Strategy and this was described in Chapter 4. Our approach was twofold. Firstly, to provide an overview of what strategy is, its importance and criticality to organizational survival. We certainly do not in any way position ourselves as strategy experts either from an academic or indeed practical leadership perspective. However, we endeavored as an overview to provide our own perspectives in this area and refer you to a vast literature which is written on this subject. Nevertheless, we hope that this cursory trip through the field was useful and gave you some insights. Strategy is of course critical because it provides the basis for Clarity and therefore an opportunity for people to understand where the organization is heading and why. However, the second theme of this chapter was also about how strategy should be done and in this context we emphasized the idea of strategy development which is involving and engaging with the stakeholders and therefore will provide a greater degree of commitment once implementation time comes around. Furthermore, as we all know, it is the people lower down in the organization who really understand how the business works and therefore not involving them in strategy development makes no sense for any organization. I guess the tone of this chapter and what we are saying now is a wonderful example of Blue 4 behaviour in the sense that on one hand it is about direction and on the other hand it is also about involvement. In terms of the development of the Five Cs, this approach will absolutely underpin the emergence of the Clarity and Commitment dimensions in terms of Climate.

Taking strategy to action is the most fundamental feature for an organization and this was the focus of Chapter 5. In terms of the route map we refer to this stage or phase as agenda. Critical to the Change Equation is enabling people to understand what the specific next steps are for them and furthermore what are the outcomes and consequences of these next steps. In essence we are talking about identifying the change agenda and therefore creating clear direction about what needs to be done. In defining the agenda the change leader needs to ensure that there is real clarity in people's minds about three things: firstly the current state, secondly the state that we are endeavoring to achieve and thirdly a detailed analysis and specification of what needs to happen in order to get from present to future requirements. While the development of strategy as a process can help individuals develop dissatisfaction with the current situation and a sense of the future, it is essentially these activities described in Chapter 5 that provide the third critical opportunity to identify what we actually have to do next and why. Again, this is an example of Blue 4 behaviour with the individual change leader involving people but this time looking at direction from a more detailed perspective.

The third critical theme is probably the most emotive and difficult issue that the change leader needs to address and in Chapter 6 we discussed the topic of Capability particularly at the level of the top team. In this we remarked on the criticality for the chief executive to ensure in their early tenure, and certainly at the beginning of any major change program, that the executive team members are actually up to the job. At a high level, we mean can these individuals successfully deliver Blue 4 behaviour? However, underpinning this we unpacked Blue 4 to reflect on the qualities required by people in these senior positions. We described a framework looking at various aspects of behaviour, process experience together with the ability to cope at the mental capacity level required in a senior position.

We cannot emphasize this enough but probably the most important thing that any chief executive or senior change leader will ever do is ensure their team members are up to the job. Those who don't achieve this always regret it within a couple of years and the few who do will always reflect on how it was this that made the difference between success and failure.

Assuming that Capability is in place or at least getting in place, the senior change leader needs to create the team in a collective sense. This is another critical theme that was discussed in Chapter 7 in terms of how to make the team work and take advantage of the necessarily diverse range of qualities that individual team members bring to the party. In this context of team building we introduced the idea of Blue 4 at the level of the team. Blue 4 behaviour in a team is collaborative. The team engages with itself effectively and at the same time is able to focus on direction and tackling the difficult issues that need to be addressed. This work is almost fundamental for any team particularly in the early stages of a change program. The authors' collective experience particularly in the field of mergers and acquisitions is that the emergence of Blue 4 style is a critical determinant of whether the new organization fully capitalizes on the previous investment.

In Chapter 8 we extended the discussion on Capability and team working to the broader organization and considered how Blue 4 behaviour development can be used in the full leadership population to help facilitate the Five Cs of Climate. We have been involved with many organizations and have seen the practical possibility and feasibility of organizations raising their Blue 4 game and how this subsequently can drive Climate and the delivery of successful change and therefore business improvement.

This is what we call a 10 20 40 game. By this we made the point that a 10% shift (improvement) in Blue 4 behaviour will give you a 20% hike in the Climate. Over time this collective enhancement of behaviour and conditions for change (i.e. the Five Cs) delivers bottom line performance improvement. We cite 40% simply because in a number of interventions we have been intimately involved with this has typically been an average of the bottom line improvements that we have observed – they do of course have a broad range of anything from 10% to 200% plus.

Implicit and indeed underpinning each of the previous five themes from the route map model is the idea of Influencing or Influencing Agenda or even as some people like to call it Stakeholder Management. In Chapter 9 through our nine-box influencing model we articulated what the behaviours of influencing from a change leader need to look like. Hopefully this was a useful way of integrating the essence of any activity is the idea of what to do, the delivery for implementation together with how you build commitment and engagement from others. We hope you find this nine-box model useful. We have found that it is particularly helpful for change leaders to reflect on what went well or not so well from their style and perspective of any change program.

All of these features are critical elements of a leader delivering change management or leadership in a Blue 4 style enabling the conditions of Climate to be established therefore overcoming the issues of the psychology of change, the Change Equation and the aspect of Cognitive Dissonance. If this can be achieved, our experience shows a far greater chance of a successful change delivery and therefore improved business performance.

Rules of the Game

To be honest, these rules are nothing earth shattering. Indeed we almost hesitate to mention them because we have often felt them to be "common sense." However, recently a client recounted that in his view the real issue was that there was much about common sense that wasn't actually too common. So, please forgive us if you think we are stating the blindingly obvious but sometimes we all need a gentle reminder.

1. Managing Change

Before we get started on reviewing what has gone before, let us spend a moment to consider the whole issue of leading change. In Chapter 1 we introduced the notion of the change leader but pretty much left it there. Who should sponsor change? Who should lead it? And does it matter?

2. Who leads change?

Anybody who works in an organization can be a change leader; the only real difference being that the magnitude of the change that can be led differs depending on where you sit in that organization. A shop floor employee can change the people with whom she works, as can a call center operator. A trade union official can work to change their own organization or one where they are represented. A mid-level manager can change their work team and, clearly, a CEO can change their company. So any of us, wherever we sit, might aspire to be or actually be a change leader.

However, as we discussed in Chapter 9 (Influencing), from wherever you are leading change, it is absolutely mission critical that you ensure you have the right support from the right people at the right time - whether this be a board of directors, a supervisor or line manager, and/or relevant external stakeholders. Sometimes gaining such support is easy and for some people it may be intuitive but at other times it requires the use of the Influencing approach we described earlier using the Influencing Model (Chapter 9). Sure there may be change management teams or champions eventually, but all change starts with someone somewhere deciding that the current state isn't good enough - somebody who is dissatisfied enough (remember the Change Equation in Chapter 1) to want to make a difference.

3. Project Management

Should it embrace formal project management principles or can it be something more organic?

Well firstly, any change program has to be tailored to reflect the nature of the organization, the type of change envisaged, its complexity and its impact versus difficulty. Thus, there is no right answer but there is certainly the best fit for any given situation. Rather than make this too complicated, the essence is that if your change is high impact then it is worth expending time and effort on the planning, and if it also carries a high degree of difficulty then it is also worth setting up a formal project or program management process. But, as always, focus first on those things that have a big benefit but which are easy to do and focus last on those things which also have a big benefit but which are really tough to do and ignore totally those ideas with small benefits which are hard to do!

4. Simplicity

Too many times people want to show that they are smart by making things complicated whereas in reality really smart people make things simple and actionable. Writing a short presentation is undoubtedly harder than writing a long one. Reducing complexity requires thought and insight; organizations often get lost in complexity, get paralyzed by analysis, and miss the point completely. When someone says to us "this is really complicated" we usually wonder whether they are telling us this because they are too stupid to understand it or they think we are! Therefore, all change leaders should work hard on getting to the essence of the problem, reducing it to actionable chunks, and ensuring that the ideas are conveyed in clear, simple, jargon-free language. We hate jargon because so often it obscures meaning and, even worse, just conceals sloppy thinking. Sure, there are technical terms that are required within industries but so much management-speak really doesn't fit into that category. Simplicity is a great aid to building Clarity. Complex language and ideas often result in divergent assumptions or understanding. Simplicity strips away the verbiage and gets to the essence in a way that all can understand.

Nor should complex language or ideas be used to disguise the reality. It rarely works, it is dishonest and most people see through such deception pretty quickly - and when they do, their resistance is usually higher than it would have been if the deception hadn't been attempted in the first place.

5. Planning

The old saying "If you want to get ahead get a plan" is very apt. The plan can be simple or relatively elaborate but having no plan or a half-baked one means flying blind - speed without velocity as we referred to it in Chapter 1. The key to success is often the thought and effort put into the planning phase. Time spent at this stage is rarely wasted and "front-end" loading by spending quality time really thinking through the plan, contingencies and fall-backs will ensure more speed once the change gathers momentum. Making sure that the plan is well specced and shared widely is also helpful because it is a final opportunity to catch any lack of alignment within the leadership team. Unfortunately, many leaders recall the phrase "Just Do It!" and take that as an invitation to charge off unthinkingly. Indeed procrastination or paralysis is not a virtue either, but skipping or skimping on the planning phase will mean less speed later on in the process. Planning is a key component of each of the Five Cs: it aids Clarity, it engenders Commitment, it ensures Consistency, and it reinforces Constancy and Capability. So, to paraphrase, "Planning – Just Do It!"

6. Organization

Organize for success. Too often organizations try to avoid the issue of ensuring that they have the right organization and people to drive change. This is usually because they wish to avoid upsetting "good" people and so they compromise on the Clarity and Consistency that the right organization with the right people creates. This is not to say that sorting these things out is easy; it is often neither easy nor pleasant but this misses the point. Leaders are paid to deliver positive change and they are not paid to be popular or populist. In Blue 4 mode (remember our Leadership Style Matrix) the leader does make the necessary changes but does so in a way that treats people with respect and preserves their dignity. That a change is going to happen is not debatable but how it happens is the aspect that shows relevant concern for the individual or team. No one likes to be fired, demoted or moved sideways and nobody likes doing this to others, but many times it simply has to be done for the overall good of the organization, its people and its stakeholders.

7. Measurement

You know the phrase "you can't manage what you don't measure" – everybody knows this phrase. One reason why organizations trip up on the Constancy component of the Five Cs is that they get distracted or sidetracked because nobody is keeping score. So why is it that often measurement doesn't take place? Without measurement you can't know where you are, whether the progress is on plan and what corrective actions are required to get back on plan or stay there. Equally, where we see measurement we often see measures that only look backward rather than forward and we also see measures that are so aggregated as to be meaningless.

Measuring the past or predicting the future? In mining, tons produced is clearly an important backward-looking metric but it becomes so much more powerful if studied in conjunction with the amount of development work undertaken to facilitate future mining. The rate and amount of development is what governs future production and so this is a much more useful future measure than tons produced last month. In consulting, the situation is similar: last month's billing is important, the future pipeline is important but the real measure of future success is the amount of origination activity. And the mining and consulting examples share an important attribute in that both development and origination are activities that are costs rather than revenues.

So when companies cut costs, if they are not using future-facing measures they may not spot people cutting out costs today that will actually drive revenue tomorrow.

8. Program/Project Management (PM)

A Program contains a number of Projects. A project is a discrete set of activities with a defined end point. Here we will simply use PM to represent both. The degree to which you need PM simply depends on the scale of the change program being managed. PM is a particular skill set - one that is clearly recognized in capital construction or IT implementation but which we believe has wider applicability for any program of complex change.

We aren't PM experts and so we simply suggest that you consider using somebody with formal PM experience if you think your change program is of sufficient complexity that it needs somebody with these skills to keep it on track.

PHEW – THAT IS IT!

We have arrived at the end! But hopefully for you it is just the beginning of a successful and fruitful change adventure. Good luck and we look forward to hearing about it!

REFERENCES

ADAMS, J.S. (1963) Toward an understanding of inequity. *Journal of Abnormal and Social Psychology*, 67, 422-436

BANDURA, A. (1997b). *Self-efficacy: The exercise of control*. Stanford: WH Freeman & Co.

BECKHARD, R. and HARRIS, R. (1987), *Organizational Transitions: Managing Complex Change*. Reading, Mass: Addison-Wesley Pub. Co.

BURKE, W.W. and LITWIN, G.H. (1992). A Causal Model of Organizational Performance and Change. *Journal of Management,* 18 (3), 523-545

CATTELL, R.B. (1946). *The description and measurement of personality.* New York, NY: World Books

CHRISTENSEN, C. M. (1997). *The Innovator's Dilemma: When New Technologies Cause Great Firms to Fail.* Harvard Business School Press

COLLINS, J. (2009) *How the Mighty Fall: And Why Some Companies Never Give In.* New York, NY: Harper Collins

COLLINS, J.C. and PORRAS, J.I. (1996). Building Your Company's Vision. *Harvard Business Review,* September/October 1996

COSTA, P.T, Jr and MCCRAE, R.R. (1976). Age differences in personality structure: A cluster analytic approach. *Journal of Gerontology*, 31 (5), 564–570

DEMING, W.E. (1982). *Out of the Crisis.* Cambridge Massachusetts: Massachusetts Institute of Technology, Center for Advanced Educational Services

DONALD C. HAMBRICK and JAMES W. FREDRICKSON (2001). Academy of Management Executive, 15, 48-59

EKVALL, G. (1987). The climate metaphor in organizational theory. In B. Bass and P. Drenth (eds.). *Advances in organizational psychology.* Beverley Hills, CA: Sage

FESTINGER, L. (1957). *A Theory of Cognitive Dissonance*. Stanford: Stanford University Press

GOLEMAN, D. (2000). Leadership that gets results. *Harvard Business Review*, April 2000

HANRETTY, C. (2014). Taxpayers of Surrey Heath unite: identifying the most left-wing and right-wing constituencies. In P. Cowley & R. Ford (eds.), *Sex, Lies and the Ballot Box: 50 things you need to know about British elections*. London, England: Biteback

HERZBERG, F., MAUSNER, B. and SNYDERMAN, B.B. (1959). *The motivation to work*. New York, NY: Wiley

JOHNSON, G. and SCHOLES, K. (2006) *Exploring Corporate Strategy: Text and Cases*. UK: Prentice Hall Ltd.

LEWIN, K., LIPPIT, R., and WHITE, R. (1939). Patterns of aggressive behaviour in experimentally created "social climates." *Journal of Social Psychology*, 10, 271-299

LEWIN, K. (1951). *Field theory in social science*. New York, NY: Harper & Row

LEWIN, K. (1947). Frontiers in Group Dynamics. In Cartwright, D (ed.). *Field Theory in Social Science*. London: Social Science Paperbacks

LITWIN, G. and STRINGER, R. (1968). *Motivation and organizational climate*. Cambridge, MA:
Harvard University Press

LOCKE, E.A. and LATHAM, G.P. (1990). *A theory of goal setting and task performance*. Englewood Cliffs, NJ: Prentice Hall

LOWE, J. (1998). *Jack Welch Speaks: Wisdom from the World's Greatest Business Leader*. UK: Wiley

MASLOW A.H. (1943). A theory of human motivation. *Psychological Review*, 50, 370-396

MCCLELLAND, D. (1987). *Human Motivation*. Cambridge, UK: Cambridge University Press

MCCRAE, R.R. and COSTA, P.T. Jr (1987). Validation of the five-factor model of personality across instruments and observers. *Journal of Personality and Social Psychology*, 52 (1), 81–90

NADLER, D. and TUSHMAN, M. (1989). Organizational Frame Bending: Principles for Managing Reorientation. *The Academy of Management Executive*, 3 (3), 194-204

OLSON, E. (2008). Achieving success in the Globalization of Leadership Development In J.L.Noel and D.L.Dotlich (eds.). *Pfeiffer Annual: Leadership Development*. (pp. 81-88) San Francisco, CA: Pfeiffer

PORTER, M. E. (1996). What is Strategy? *Harvard Business Review*, November/December 1996

PORTER, M.E. (1979). How Competitive Forces Shape Strategy. *Harvard Business Review*, March/April 1979

PORTER, M.E. (2008). The Five Competitive Forces That Shape Strategy. *Harvard Business Review*, January 2008

PRAHALAD, C.K., and HAMEL, G. (1990). The Core Competence of the Corporation. *Harvard Business Review*, May/June 1990

RUMELT, R. (2011). *Good Strategy Bad Strategy: The Difference and Why It Matters*. UK: Crown Business

SCHEIN, E.H. (1996). Kurt Lewin's change theory in the field and in the classroom: notes towards a model of management learning. *Systems Practice*, 9 (1), 25-47

SHAW, G. B., (1903) *Man and superman*. Westminster: Archibald Constable and Co. Ltd.

SKINNER, B.F. (1938). *The behaviour of organisms: an experimental analysis*. Oxford, UK: Appleton Century

THURSTONE, L.L. (1934). The Vectors of Mind. *Psychological Review*, *41, 1-32*

TUCKMAN, B. (1965). Developmental sequence in small groups. *Psychological Bulletin, 63, (6) 384-399*

TZU, S. (2002). *The Art of War.* Dover Edition. Mineola, NY: Dover Publications, Inc.

VROOM, V.H. (1964) *Work Motivation.* New York: Wiley & Sons

ELECTRONIC AND WEB RESOURCES

Apollo 13 [DVD], 1995. Directed by Ron HOWARD. USA: Universal Pictures and Imagine Entertainment

ASHTON, J. (2009). Cameron Clyne: The banker who swims with sharks [online]. *The Sunday Times, 19th April.* Available from: http://www.thesundaytimes.co.uk/sto/Migration/article162098.ece [Accessed on 20th March 2011]

FORD, H. Good Reads (n.d.) [viewed 2012-04-11]. Henry Ford Quotes. *Good Reads* [online]. Good Reads Inc. Available from: http://www.goodreads.com/author/quotes/203714.Henry_Ford

Glowinkowski International Limited. (2009). GPI™ Consultant's Manual [online]. Available from: http://www.glowinkowski.com/GPI-Technical-Manual.html

JACOBS, E. (2010). 20 Questions, Barbara Stocking, Oxfam [online]. The Financial Times, 17th June. Available from: http://www.ft.com/cms/s/0/99fac454-7a38-11df-aa69-00144feabdc0.html#axzz2POzCn5H1 [Accessed on 17th June 2010]

KENNEDY, John, Fitzgerald, 1961-01-20. *"Ask not what your country can do for you" – Inaugural Address. BBC History* [online]. Available from: http://www.bbc.co.uk/history/worldwars/coldwar/kennedy_audio.shtml

SHAW, G.B. (1903). Man and Superman *"Maxims: Reason" Oxford Essential Quotations* [online]. Oxford, UK: Oxford University Press. Available from: http://www.oxfordreference.com/view/10.1093/acref/9780191735240.001.0001/q-oro00009969

ABOUT THE AUTHORS

Russell King

Russell is an experienced business leader and company director.

For over 30 years, Russell worked with large multinational blue-chip companies ICI and Anglo American in human resources, business development, marketing, business leadership and strategy roles.

At Anglo, he was a member of the Executive Committee and was responsible for HR and business development globally before running global strategy development as its Chief Strategy Officer.

Currently, Russell is chairman of Hummingbird Resources and SID of Aggreko plc, and a NED of Interserve plc, Sepura plc and Spectris plc. At Aggreko and Spectris he chairs their Remuneration Committees. He is a senior advisor to Heidrick & Struggles's EMEA CEO and Board Practice. Russell is a senior advisor to Glowinkowski International Ltd.

Steve Glowinkowski PhD

Steve is a consultant and research psychologist. His main focus is assessment of senior leaders and their teams. In terms of early career, Steve spent ten years in a variety of senior change roles in the Chemical and Financial Service sectors.

In the early 1990s Steve established the consultancy Glowinkowski International Ltd. This operates across most sectors and has been active in Europe, Africa, Asia Pacific and North and South America. Steve has also developed a range of tools and techniques together with an implementation approach which enables organizations to develop their behaviours and improve performance.

Steve has published a variety of academic and business material. He is Honorary Professor at the University of Essex and visiting Professor at the University of Glyndŵr. Steve is also co-founder and chairman of the Gillson Partnership which is a consulting and talent analytics firm based in Southern California.